Copyright

The characters and events portrayed in this book are fictitious. Any similarity to real persons, living or dead, is coincidental and not intended by the author.

No part of this book may be reproduced, or stored in a retrieval system, or transmitted in any form or by any means, electronic, mechanical, photocopying, recording, or otherwise, without express written permission of the publisher.

ISBN-13: 979-8-6839-4810-8

Cover design by: Avanska
Printed in the United States of America

CONTENTS

Copyright

Foreword

Disclaimer

How To Use This Book   1

SECTION I: BACKPACKS   5

1. Day Packs   6

2. Multi-day packs   15

SECTION II: CAMPING   26

3. Tents   27

4. Sleeping Bags   39

5. Sleeping Bag Liners   51

6. Sleeping Pads   56

SECTION III: COOKING   66

7. Stoves   67

8. Cookware   76

9. Utensils   83

10. Cleaning Items   86

SECTION IV: WATER	91
11. Water Storage	92
12. Water Treatment	98
SECTION V: NAVIGATION	108
13. Compasses	109
14. GPS Devices	116
15. Watches	124
SECTION VI: ACCESSORIES	130
16. Trekking Poles	131
17. Headlamps	141
18. Binoculars	148
19. Chargers	157
20. Knives and Multi-Tools	165
21. Cameras	179
SECTION VII: SAFETY	186
22. First Aid Kits	187
23. Foot Care	193
24. Repair Kits	200
25. Communication Devices	204
SECTION VIII: HYGIENE	216
26. Camp Bathrooms	217
27. Feminine Hygiene	222
SECTION IX: CHECKLISTS	226
28. Summer Day-Hike	227

29. Winter Day-Hike	230
30. Summer Overnight Hike	233
31. Winter Overnight Hike	237
32. Summer Multi-Day Hike	241
33. Winter Multi-Day Hike	245
Write A Review	249
Next Steps	251
Books In This Series	255
About The Author	257
About The Adventure Junkies	259
Photo Credits	263

FOREWORD

Back in 2014, we created The Adventure Junkies to be THE place to go to learn about outdoor activities and connect with a global network of like-minded people.

Over the years, we've received countless emails and messages from people from all around the world who want an answer to the same question: "What gear do I really need to go hiking and what's optional?"

Nowadays there is an excessive amount of information about hiking going around the internet. Instead of making things easier, it makes people confused. Some companies try to scare beginner hikers into buying a long list of expensive equipment. They do this by telling them that the more gear they have, the safer they will be in the outdoors. But do you really need all that? How do you know what's essential and what's luxury as a beginner?

The gear you need to go for a 5-hour hike is very different from the gear you need for a week-long backpacking trip in the mountains. But how can you know the difference if you've never hiked before?

Then there's the difference between "need" and "want." Some pieces of gear are absolutely essential to go hiking while others simply increase your safety or comfort and are just nice to have. When you're first getting started, we know that you just want to get your feet wet and see if you really enjoy hiking before investing in all the gear. How can you do that in a world where magazines, salesmen, and websites are constantly telling you that you need a long list of expensive equipment? What gear should you buy first and what can wait for later?

That's why we created this book. Our goal is simple. To answer the one question we've been asked the most over the years: "What gear do you actually need to go hiking, and what's just nice to have?"

In this book, you will find out exactly what you need to pack and how to choose the right equipment for your next – or first – hiking adventure.

We hope you enjoy this book and we'll see you on the trail!

Antonio Cala & Amanda Zeisset

Co-Founders of The Adventure Junkies

DISCLAIMER

The information contained in this book is for informational purposes only. Any advice that we give is our opinion based on our own experience. You should always seek the advice of a professional before acting on something that we have published or recommended.

The material in this book may include information, products or services by third parties. Third Party Materials comprise the products and opinions expressed by their owners. As such, we do not assume responsibility or liability for any Third-Party material or opinions. The publication of such Third-Party Materials does not constitute our guarantee of any information, instruction, opinion, products or services contained within the Third-Party Material.

No part of this publication shall be reproduced, transmitted, or sold in whole or in part in any form, without the prior written consent of The Adventure Junkies LLC. All trademarks and registered trademarks appearing in this guide are the property of their respective owners.

By reading this guide, you agree that ourselves

and our company is not responsible for whatever might happen due the decisions made relating to any information presented in this guide.

HOW TO USE THIS BOOK

This book is meant to be used as a resource for both new and experienced hikers. Rather than reading it cover-to-cover, it is suggested to use this book as a reference guide.

Section 2 covers a variety of hikes one may take, ranging from day hikes to multi-day trips in conditions from summer to winter. Use this section as your starting point and refer to the appropriate checklist when preparing and packing for a trip.

The checklists are designed to give you an idea of which pieces of gear are essential (that is, what's non-negotiable and must be brought with you) and which items are optional. Keep in mind that the optional gear we've included will either increase your safety, increase your comfort, or both.

When considering what additional items to bring for your trip, take into consideration the location of your trip, the time of year, the forecasted weather, your experience level with hiking, your familiarity with the trail you'll be hiking, and what you personally prefer for creature comforts.

This will help you better customize the checklists to your personal needs.

For example, a GPS unit is always an optional resource but will greatly increase your safety on the trail. The longer your trips and the more unfamiliar the territory you're hiking, the more you should consider bringing one as a backup in case you get lost.

Keep in mind that it is your responsibility to ensure that you are properly equipped and prepared for the hikes you take. It is always better to err on the side of caution than to introduce unnecessary risk into your adventures. Hiking and backpacking will always have an inherent risk, but that risk can be minimized and managed with the right preparation.

When considering creature comforts to bring along (i.e. items that aren't essential but will increase your comfort), think about what you may need to make your experience more enjoyable. Backpacking doesn't require you to be the most ultralight, primitive, camping commando that ever was (unless you're into that). Instead, it's about making strategic trade-offs while balancing overall pack weight with items you need.

For example, a camp chair is not an essential item, but will greatly increase your comfort. Many people find that bringing a lightweight trail stool is well worth the extra 18 oz., especially those who may have some minor back pain after a full day of hiking. Strategic "comfort" choices such as this will make your experience more about thriving rather than merely surviving.

Moving to Section 3, you'll find chapters diving into specific gear items such as backpacks, first aid kits, and water filtration systems. Section 3 is divided into 8 overarching categories that will help you find particular chapters more easily:

Backpacks
Camping
Cooking
Water
Navigation
Accessories
Safety
Hygiene

Within each chapter, there are 4 major sections that will help you better understand the piece of gear being covered. You may read the chapter in its entirety or use it as a reference, skipping to the sections that you feel you need the most information on. The 4 sections of each chapter are, in order:

1. Do You Really Need It?
This section gives a brief explanation of why a piece of gear is essential or, if not essential, why you may want to consider having it.

2. Things to Consider
This is a broad section that varies based upon the

topic. Typically, the section will cover the most prominent features to look for when buying that item.

3. Techie Language Explained

This book does its best to use as simple and plain English as possible, yet sometimes it's impossible to avoid using gear-specific terminology. For such occasions, this section is a quick reference glossary of terms you may not be familiar with. Refer to this section as necessary when reading through the chapter.

4. Product Recommendations

If you're looking for a few quick recommendations for a piece of gear, skip to this section. You'll find 5 product recommendations each with a different type of person in mind ranging from female hikers to minimalist enthusiasts, and from budget-conscious types to gear junkies.

We at The Adventure Junkies hope you find this to be an invaluable resource when planning for your next hiking adventure! For more information on topics not specifically covered in this book, check out our website theadventurejunkies.com. Happy Hiking!

SECTION I: BACKPACKS

1. DAY PACKS

If you want to get the most out of a proper day hike, snagging a day pack is pretty essential. It doesn't have to be the most expensive pack or sport a lot of fancy bells and whistles, but having a convenient place to store your gear while hiking is a necessity.

Consider what type of hiking you'll be doing and what items you may want to bring along. Will your hike last several hours or take up the better part of the day? Then you'll definitely need a day pack to hold your lunch and keep a bottle of water handy to stay hydrated. If you think the sun may drop before you make it back to your car, having a day pack will make it much simpler to carry a headlamp to safely navigate the trail hands-free and an extra layer to stay warm in the evening.

Things To Consider When Choosing A Day Pack

1. Frame Type and Weight

Frameless
Without the internal support of a frame, frameless backpacks are perfect for you if you plan to carry a lighter load. With a few essentials in the bag, frameless day packs are suitable for lightweight enthusiasts and short, casual hikes.

Without a frame, the overall weight of these day packs drops considerably. The low weight of an empty frameless backpack means less weight to carry over the course of your hike.

Internal Frame
Day packs that sport an internal frame do an outstanding job of supporting heavier loads. Due to their rigid construction, they're able to keep their shape and are better suited for long distance treks.

The weight of the pack when empty, known as the base weight, of internal frame day packs tends to be in the range of 2 – 3 lbs, adding considerable weight to your overall hike. However, this may be a necessary trade-off to ensure you're able to pack all the gear you need and still be comfortable on your hike while carrying the pack on your back.

2. Gear Capacity

When figuring out the right day pack for you, how much gear it can hold will be a big factor. Consider what you will you most likely want to bring as well as what type of hiking you intend to do.

Extra Small (10 Liters or Less)
If you only plan on hiking short distances in good weather or you prefer to tackle day hikes in an ultralight manner, consider purchasing a smaller day pack. Bags of this size are ideal for carrying a few essential items, such as your car keys, a light jacket, a small snack, and sunglasses.

Small (11 – 20 Liters)
Day packs of this size allow you to carry a slightly larger number of items than a small day pack and typically come with side pockets for stowing water bottles or stashing easy-access gear like your sunglasses or sunscreen. With a pack this size, you can throw in an extra layer for when the temperature drops or pack a lunch for a picnic at your favorite overlook!

Medium (21 – 36 Liters)

As the most commonly used size, day packs in this range allow you to maximize your carrying capacity without overpacking. An extra layer, food, hammocks, and more will all fit for a full day of adventuring. Bonus: most packs of this size offer hydration bladder reservoirs that don't impede your storage space, so you'll stay hydrated for your entire hike!

Large (36 – 50 Liters)
Best for intense hiking situations such as winter or extreme weather, packs of this size can accommodate a host of gear including compact stoves, first aid kits, water filtration systems, and multiple clothing layers. Day packs this large are also great for parents who may need to carry items for their children.

3. Pack Access

Day packs are crafted with a variety of uses in mind and the type of access a pack provides will depend on the activity, weather, and particular needs of each hiker.

Top
Classic and simple, the top loading day pack is designed to keep quick access items near the top. Items that don't need to be accessed until later in the day, like an extra layer when the sun sets, are kept at the bottom.

Panel

Most commonly used in day packs, access to the main compartment is obtained via a U-shaped zipper that allows a panel to fold away. These are great for snagging gear quickly and grabbing items deeper in the pack.

Front

Usually paired with Top or Panel access, Front loading day packs provide full access to all gear, top to bottom. This makes it easy to re-organize on-the-go or to snag bottom-of-the-bag items without completely unloading your pack.

Side

Although not commonly found, side access packs can be a good choice for those needing gear divided into top and bottom compartments. Typically mated with Top or Panel access, Side access day packs are great for photographers who need to safely stash a camera or hikers who need quick access to a first aid kit.

4. Pockets and Gear Loops

How to decide how many pockets you need in your day pack can only be determined by your hiking style and what you need access to. Need to quickly grab a protein bar without stopping to rummage through your pack? You'll want stash pockets on your hip belt. Or do you need a smaller pocket so your Chapstick and keys don't get lost at the bottom of the main compartment? Consider a pack that has a small zip near the top.

Gear loops can also provide quick access for items that may not fit in your bag, like an ice pick or a camera tripod. You can also lash sandals for water crossings and secure water bottles to the outside of the pack with a carabiner attached to the gear loops (sometimes called a daisy chain). Just be careful not to overdo it, as too much gear hooked to the front of your pack can swing around and make it more difficult to hike.

Techie Language Explained

Stash Pocket: A small zippered pocket that can be found on the hip belt, near the top of the bag, or even inside larger pockets. These storage compartments help keep small items from getting lost.

Side Pocket: Auxiliary pockets that typically flank either side of the pack and don't have zippers. These are good for storing a water bottle, camera tripod, ground pad, and more.

Tool Loop: An exterior loop that allows hikers to lash tools and gear to the outside of their bag.

Hip Belt: Found on most day packs, the hip belt is

essential for creating ergonomic comfort by reducing the load from your shoulders and sharing it with your hips.

Hydration Reservoir Pouch: Many day packs include a slim pouch that runs the entire length of the bag that is dedicated to holding a hydration reservoir. Sold separately, a hydration reservoir can allow you to carry anywhere between 1 – 3 liters of water in a slim, low profile design that reduces the bulk and weight of standard water bottles. Hydration reservoirs also have a tube that attaches to the day pack's shoulder strap, allowing you to drink water on-the-go without needing to stop and take off the pack to grab your water bottle.

Rain Cover: If you have a potential of getting caught in the rain on your day hike, a good rain cover for your pack will help keep your valuables dry. Some companies, such as Osprey and REI, almost always include a rain cover with a specific storage pouch on their day packs. If the particular model of day pack you choose doesn't include a rain cover, you can always purchase one separately.

Load Lifter Straps: Positioned near the top of the pack, load lifter straps connect your pack's shoulder straps to the body of the pack in order to create ergonomic comfort. For the best fit, adjust the straps at a 45-degree angle to the pack.

Ventilated Back Panel: Many day packs include a ventilated back panel to increase airflow between the bag and your back. The added ventilation reduces back sweat and contributes to a more comfortable hike.

Product Recommendations

If you're a casual hiker who goes hiking 2-3 times per year, the *Osprey Talon 11* is a great option for you. With a capacity of 11L and 6 exterior pockets, it's not a huge pack, but you'll still have an ample amount of space to stash your gear.

Serious hikers who are hitting the trail once or twice a month will find a great fit with the *Patagonia Nine Trails 28L*. Its generous 28 liters of storage gives you plenty of space to fit a variety of gear while the wide opening main compartment gives you easy access to your belongings without exploding your pack on the trail.

For the adventurous woman needing a trusty companion to conquer any trail, *Osprey's Sirrus 24* provides organization and convenience with tactical flair. Boasting 7 pockets and multiple gear loops, this pack offers supreme customization with a fit designed just for women.

Gear junkies who need an ample amount of room and quick access to gear at a moment's notice will find the *Mystery Ranch Scree 32* a suitable fit. Two rows of daisy chains provide endless options when lashing gear to the outside of the pack, and its adjustable tool loops ensure your gear won't get lost on the trail.

If you're the type of hiker that pushes the boundaries in extreme environments, there's no better day pack than the *REI Trail 40*. As a Winter Hiker needing to fit multiple layers, a rain jacket, compact stove, water filtration system, first aid kit, and more, you'll find this pack performs beyond expectations.

To get the most up-to-date information, please visit our web article *Best Day Hiking Backpacks* where you'll find the latest day pack recommendations. This list is updated every year.

2. MULTI-DAY PACKS

A quality multi-day pack is one of the most essential items any backpacker, hiker, camper, or adventurer needs. It is your command center. The ability to pack, stash, and store your gear and then take it on the go is crucial for a successful adventure. From thy backpack, all things are possible.

Things To Consider When Choosing

Multi-Day Packs

1. Gear Capacity

Choosing the proper size multi-day pack is the biggest decision you'll make, as the size of your pack will affect how many days you're able to stay on the trail. Consider when you'll most likely be hiking, as winter backpacking will require much more room than summer camping.

30 – 50 Liters
Best suited for weekend trips, a multi-day pack in this range will comfortably pack enough gear for 1 – 3 days in late spring, summer, and early fall.

Depending on the type of gear you bring and how light you can pack, you may be able to extend this by an extra day or two. For example, summers have better conditions for sleeping in a hammock. Carrying a hammock instead of a tent would significantly reduce your overall pack weight. It would also leave room in the pack for other essentials like more food and water, allowing you to stay out longer.

50 – 70 Liters
Considered the most widely used type of backpack, these multi-day packs will comfortably extend your trip to the 3 – 5-day range. For winter backpackers, packs of this size will accommodate overnight and even 2-night trips.

The best thing about packs in this range is that they can be "sized down" to also be useful for weekend summer trips. Keep in mind that using a pack of this size for a shorter weekend trip in warm weather requires great discipline when packing, as it's easy to fill the extra space with unnecessary items. You don't want to carry a pack that's uncomfortably heavy just because you couldn't decide what to leave at home!

70+ Liters

Multi-day packs that exceed 70 liters are best for extended trips that last a minimum of 5 nights. The sheer size of these packs will ensure that you're able to bring enough supplies for the long haul.

Packs in this range are great for families with young children. With a 70+ Liter pack, you'll be able to carry your children's supplies as well as your own.

70+ Liter packs are also in high demand for winter treks lasting more than 2 nights. You'll be able to haul thicker clothing, more layers, and larger, winter sleeping bags without worrying about running out of space.

2. Size

Torso Length

The most important measurement for choosing the correct size multi-day pack is measuring the length of your torso. To do this, you will need a flexible measuring tape and a helping hand from a friend or relative.

Your torso length can be determined by measuring the distance between your C7 vertebra at the base of your neck and your iliac crest at the top of your hip bones. Start by tilting your head forward. You want to feel for a bony bump on the back of your neck (the place where your neck and shoulders meet, AKA the C7 vertebra). This is your starting point.

Next, put your hands on your hips (at your waistline) and slide them down to the tops of your hip bones with thumbs pointing towards your back. Now draw an imaginary line between your thumbs. This is your stopping point.

Last, using a measuring tape, have your partner measure the distance from the starting point down to the imaginary line on your hips. This is the length of your torso. Use the chart below to determine what size multi-day pack you will need based upon your measurement.

Torso length depending on the pack size:
extra small: up to 15"
small: 16" – 17"
medium/regular: 18" – 19"
large/tall: 20" +

It's also important to note that most multi-day packs come with an adjustable suspension for torso length. This is designed for users to dial in the perfect length. Each brand has its own system – check the instructions on the pack for sizing adjustments.

Waist Size

Although the proper size of a multi-day pack can usually be found with just the torso length, make sure to measure your waist size as well. Compare your waist measurement to the hip belt size on your chosen pack to make sure they match. If they don't, double check to see if you can swap out the hip belt for a smaller or larger one. Most brands are willing to do this at no extra cost.

Waist measurement is also a good tiebreaker for those who may fall in-between sizes. For example, if your torso measurement is somewhere between 19" – 20", it can be difficult to decide whether to size up or down. In this case, check your waist size. If you have average sized or narrower hips, size down to the Medium/Regular pack size. If you have wider than average hips, size up to ensure the hip belt will properly fit. In either case, the torso length can be adjusted up or down to ensure a snug fit.

Hip Belt

The first point of adjustment after donning your pack is the hip belt. Multi-day packs are designed to reduce stress and pressure from your shoulders by redirecting the weight to your hips. This creates ergonomic comfort on long hikes.

To properly adjust the hip belt, put on the backpack while fully loaded with gear and clip the hip belt buckle. Ensure the padded portions of the hip belt fit snugly on your hip bones. To adjust the fit, tighten the straps on either side until snug.

When fully tightened, the straps should have at least 1" of clearance between the buckle and the plastic adjustment pulley. If there is less than 1", contact the manufacturer to see if a smaller belt is available.

Shoulder Straps

The next thing you want to adjust when you first put your pack on is the shoulder straps. To tighten them, pull down and back on the strap. Be careful not to over-tighten these straps, as you don't want them to cause discomfort by digging into your shoulders. The anchor points (the place on the pack where the shoulder straps come out from) should rest 1 – 2 inches below the tops of your shoulders, just about at the top of your shoulder blades.

The shoulder straps should fit snugly without adding any weight or pressure to your shoulders. If this isn't the case, double check your hip belt to ensure the load is being supported there. If the hip belt is loaded and tightened correctly, double check the torso length, as the suspension may need to be re-adjusted.

Load Lifter Straps

Load lifter straps are a secondary point of adjust-ment after the hip belt and shoulder straps. Located near the top of the pack, they help add ergonomic comfort by assisting the shoulder straps. In order to achieve the best fit, adjust the load lifter anchor points at a 45-degree angle to the pack.

The shoulder straps should still be snug with your body after you tighten down the load lifter straps. If you find that there is a gap or separation between the shoulder straps and your body, loosen the load lifters. Over-tightened load lifter straps can pinch your shoulders over time, even if they felt good after the initial tightening. Don't be afraid to play around with the adjustment of these straps the first few times you wear your pack, until you find a comfortable and reliable snugness.

Sternum Strap

The sternum strap is a small strap near the top of your pack that comes across your chest. An optional adjustment, buckling the sternum strap can help create additional support. To dial in the right fit, slide the sternum strap up until it is about an inch below your collar bones. Buckle and tighten the strap to a snug fit without over-tightening. Some prefer to hike without this strap buckled. Experiment to see what you like best.

3. Additional Features

Removable Top Lid

Multi-day packs in the 50+ Liter size range will sometimes come with a removable top lid that can double as a day pack or hip belt pack. These can be extremely useful for those who plan to set up a base camp for multiple days. Having a removable top lid will free you from carrying your big pack on small day trips within your backpacking/camping trip.

If you've opted for a 50+ Liter pack but find yourself on a shorter trip of 1 – 3 days, a removable top lid can also be left at home to trim down on pack size/weight.

Sleeping Bag Compartment
Some multi-day packs offer additional access to the main compartment via a zipper at the bottom. This bottom compartment allows you to easily reach your sleeping bag without completely unloading everything else in your pack. Keep an eye on this feature as it helps you stay organized.

Hydration Reservoir Pouch
Most, if not all, multi-day packs now include a slim pouch in the back of the pack that can hold a hydration reservoir. Typically sold separately, some brands (such as Osprey and REI) will include a 1.5 or 2-Liter hydration reservoir at no extra cost. Hydration reservoirs (often called "bladders" or referred to by the trademarked name "CamelBak") are a fantastic alternative to bulky and heavy water bottles.

Hydration reservoirs deliver water via a tube that attaches to the shoulder straps, allowing you to drink water on the go without having to stop and unhook your water bottle.

Rain Cover

Having a rain cover for your pack can save your gear from getting totally soaked in a sudden downpour. No one likes a wet sleeping bag!

Some multi-day packs come with their own rain cover, such as those made by Osprey and REI, and have a dedicated storage pouch. These integrated rain covers are easy to deploy in case of a sudden rainstorm and can also be packed away quickly and efficiently. If your chosen multi-day pack doesn't include a rain cover, we suggest picking one up for a small cost.

Techie Language Explained

Stash Pocket: A zippered pocket that can accommodate a couple of small items, such as a protein bar or a headlamp. Most hip belts have one on each side and some multi-day packs offer a few stash pockets in the top lid (AKA "brain") for easy access.

Side Pocket: Flanking either side of the backpack, side pockets are always open and can store tent poles, trekking poles, or even a large water bottle.

Side Compression Straps: Usually found near the

side pockets, these handy straps can be tightened to pull a backpack's load closer to the frame. Doing so creates a better center of gravity for the hiker. They can also be utilized in conjunction with the side pockets to help hold onto longer items such as tent poles.

Tool Loop: A loop found on the bottom of a multi-day pack that can accommodate extra gear, external to the main compartment. These are usually used to strap on a ground pad or tarp.

Ventilated Back Panel: All multi-day packs offer some type of ventilated back panel that helps increase the air flow between the load and your back. This feature helps keep you cool and prevents your sweat from drenching your gear.

Product Recommendations

Weekend warriors who keep their adventures in the 1 – 3-day range will find a trusty hauler in the *REI Flash 45*. Sporting a modest 45L, this multi-day pack hits the sweet spot in terms of room and agility. It also boasts a smart design with unique features such as a forward angled water bottle pocket for grab'n'go accessibility.

Serious outdoor enthusiasts who are looking to spend up to 5 nights in the backcountry should consider the *Osprey Rook 65*. Its straightforward design simplifies the packing process and can accommodate an internal hydration reservoir up to a whopping 3 Liters.

Women who enjoy spending multiple days on the trail will find a great match in the *Osprey Aura AG 50*. At 50 Liters, it sits right at the cusp of 3-day adventures. This pack will provide luxurious and ample room for 1 – 3-day trips, and can easily be utilized for 3 – 5-day treks if one packs lightly.

Hikers that prefer to establish a basecamp for several days and make shorter day hikes from there will benefit from grabbing the *Osprey Aether AG 70*. The removable top lid converts into a day pack while the 70 Liter main bag will more than suffice for all your gear.

Winter backpackers looking to carry enough warmth to stay on the trail for multiple days should take a serious look at the *Mystery Ranch Terraframe 80*. The frame is sturdy enough to support loads into the 75 – 80-lb range and it has pockets and gear loops galore to stash all those extras.

To get the most up-to-date information, please visit our web article Best Backpacks for Hiking, where you'll find the latest multi-day pack recommendations. This list is updated every year.

SECTION II: CAMPING

3. TENTS

Although a tent can be an optional accessory when camping at certain times of the year, more often than not you'll want a shelter to keep you warm and dry. A good tent provides protection from any weather you might experience while camping and can be a good first defense against potential animal attacks in the wilderness as well. Just make sure you store your food properly while in the backcountry and don't plan on sleeping with your food in your tent!

If you're an ultra-light enthusiast, you might

prefer to use a hammock or tarp to lighten the load of your shelter while hiking. But if you're just car camping for the weekend or backpacking casually a few times a year, the benefits of having a tent on the trail far outweigh the potential weight savings in your pack.

And remember that if you're hiking with friends and you plan on sharing a tent, the cost of weight goes down dramatically as the tent components can be distributed evenly among your crew!

Things To Consider When Choosing A Tent

1. Capacity

Most backpacking tents can comfortably sleep between 1 – 4 people. The number of sleepers a tent can hold is known as the tent's capacity. There are several things you should keep in mind when considering the capacity of the tent you plan to purchase.

Most tents are designed to sleep exactly the number of people specified with no extra room. Consider how much gear you plan to pack with you as well as your sleeping style and your potential companions (2-legged or four!).

Sleepers who require extra elbow room or who

sprawl out at night may want to add +1 person to their expected tent size. Also, if you plan on hiking with a pet or want to have plenty of space for your backpack in the tent, then upsizing the capacity is recommended.

If you're a solo backpacker needing some extra space and have no extra companions, it may be more cost and weight effective to look for a 1-person tent in a wide or plus model. And if you're hiking or camping solo with your dog, we suggest opting for a 2-person tent – pups can take up a lot of precious space!

While couples may be fine with a snug fit in a 2-person tent, friends sharing a tent may want to opt for a 3-person tent to allow for extra space. If you're a family with children, then we recommend looking for at least a 4-person tent. And if you have four people total plus gear and pets, then we definitely suggest considering buying a 6-person tent to make sure everyone has plenty of space to sleep at night.

2. Seasonality

Tents are made with a few different "seasonality" ratings depending on the weather in which it will primarily be used. While most campers and backpackers prefer to use 3-season tents, there are some cases where an extended or 4-season option is certainly needed.

3-Season
Made to handle most seasons and weather conditions, 3-season tents will keep you comfortably covered through spring, summer, and fall. Lightweight and dependable, these tents are designed to shield you from bugs and moderate weather including rain, light snow, and modest winds. Anything beyond these limits will require a heavier duty tent.

Extended Season
Also known as 3+ season tents, these in-between models offer more strength and warmth than their 3-season counterparts. By employing an extra tent pole or two, adding more fabric layers to zippered seams, and reducing mesh fabrics, extended season tents offer added protection in early spring and late fall when unexpected snows or unseasonably low temperatures may surprise you.

Extended season tents are also a great option for those who backpack and camp at higher elevations where intense bouts of wind and snow are more likely. However, if extreme weather such as strong winds and heavy snow are expected, an upgrade to a 4-season tent is highly recommended.

4-Season
Designed to tackle harsh conditions like heavy snow and strong winds, 4-season tents employ heavy duty fabrics and more tent poles than 3-sea-

son and extended season tents to increase durability, comfort, and warmth. Also known as mountaineering tents, these shelters are created with a dome style to keep snow from accumulating on the roof and deflect extreme winds.

And extra warmth doesn't exclude 4-season tents from summer use. Removing the rainfly will allow these types of tents to breathe and increase airflow during hot summer nights.

3. Additional Features

Style
Dome Style: Best suited for all types of backpacking due to their lighter weight and thoughtfully engineered design, dome style tents have sloping walls to deflect wind and curved tops to prevent rain and snow from collecting.

Cabin Style: Better suited for families and those staying put for a few nights, cabin style tents offer more "livable" space and tend to be larger. Some models can include dividers for privacy to create multiple rooms within the dwelling. Because they are larger, heavier, and have flat roofs, these are best used in pleasant weather and as a base camp. Packing up and traveling with these tents night after night will become cumbersome.

Rainfly
Rainflies do more than just keep sudden rain showers off you while you're sleeping – they can

also help insulate your shelter by trapping warm air and prevent winds from creating a chill in your tent. They're also a good way to keep you dry by preventing morning dew from collecting on you and your belongings.

Doors & Vestibule
When sharing a tent with other people, the number of doors and their placement can help create easy access for bathroom breaks without disturbing your tent-mates.

The addition of a vestibule outside the tent doors is also a useful feature. Typically built into the rainfly, a vestibule is an extended bit of fabric that adds extra covered space separate from the main tent. This is a highly desirable feature as it can act as a "garage" to store muddy, dirty, and/or wet gear such as hiking boots. You may also choose to store your pack in the vestibule on a dry night to give you extra space inside the tent for stretching out and relaxing.

Ventilation
Mesh fabric is primarily used as a way to ventilate camping shelters. Some tents include a removable rainfly that allows the mesh to breathe and create more airflow. Other tent designs include flaps built into the tent that can be propped up to increase ventilation.

We all know that ventilation is important for creating a cooler atmosphere in warm weather. But did you know that proper ventilation can also help keep you warm in cold temperatures by reducing condensation? When you breathe and move in your tent, warm air is trapped. The colder outside air can create condensation that gets you and your gear wet. Properly ventilating your tent in cooler weather will help keep you cozy and dry!

4. Optional Accessories

Footprint
A footprint is a ground cloth that provides an extra layer between the tent's floor and the ground. It can help reduce wear and tear on the tent floor, allowing it to last longer and eliminate the need for repairs. Footprints are also useful in preventing groundwater and excess moisture from soaking your tent's floor and subsequently you and your belongings.

Many, if not most, tents have an option to purchase a custom-fitted footprint. Although you could create your own, we suggest buying a matching footprint for your tent to obtain a perfect fit. A footprint that's too big will stick out from beneath the tent and capture water, soaking your floor in the process. If it's too small, only a limited portion of your tent floor will be protected from the wet ground and you're more likely to end up wet if the whole bottom of your tent isn't covered by the footprint.

Gear Loft

Usually found as a built-in accessory on most tents, a gear loft offers extra space overhead to store quick-access items such as your car keys or a headlamp for midnight bathroom breaks. Gear lofts can also be purchased separately with additional features, such as pockets and gear loops.

Tent Repair Kit
We highly recommend including a tent repair kit with the purchase of your tent, considering how lightweight and inexpensive they are. Usually consisting of an extra swatch or two of fabric, adhesive glue, a tent pole splint, extra zippers, and a sewing needle and thread among other items, a tent repair kit can mend holes, tears, rips, broken poles, and busted zippers. It can mean the difference between a wet and dry tent or the ability to keep bugs out.

Minimalist Alternatives

For those who prefer to pack and hike as light as possible, these alternatives will provide a modest amount of shelter with reduced weight. However, be aware that hiking with ultralight gear comes with trade-offs in comfort and livability. Most of the options below are best suited for warmer weather and cannot replicate the wind protection and warmth provided by a proper tent in winter months.

1. Fly & Footprint

If your tent comes with a rainfly and a footprint, and the weather permits, you can ditch the main tent body in favor of a lighter setup. Utilizing the tent poles as a frame, you can stay covered with the rainfly and relatively dry from groundwater using the footprint (should it rain). This option, however, does leave you more exposed to potential critters joining your slumber.

2. Tarp Shelter

For ultralight adventurers that don't require the creature comforts of a traditional tent, setting up an A-frame style shelter using trekking poles will keep the morning dew off you and keep you dry during a light drizzle.

3. Hammock System

An outstanding lightweight alternative for the solo adventurer, a hammock system offers the same protections as a traditional tent. Sporting bug nets and a rainfly to stay dry, hammocks can provide better sleep than ground dwelling.

4. Bivy Sack

Short for bivouac, a bivy sack is like an extra water-resistant layer that slips over your sleeping bag. It provides protection from bugs and can add

10° – 15° degrees of warmth to your sleeping bag. However, these do not stand up well to rain and condensation.

5. Bug Shelter

Similar to a bivy sack, a bug shelter slips over your sleeping bag but will not protect against rain or morning dew. These are best suited to warm environments.

Techie Language Explained

Guyout Loops: These loops are found on the exterior of a tent or rainfly and allow small ropes called guy lines to be attached. Guy lines help to keep your tent and rainfly taut and prevents them from flapping in the wind. A properly anchored guy line can also help prevent condensation inside your tent by creating a layer of air between the two materials of the tent body and its corresponding rainfly.

Tent Pole: Lightweight plastic or metal poles that snap into place to create a frame for the tent. Tent poles create structure and stability for the tent. Some lightweight backpacking tents allow you to use trekking poles instead of proper tent poles to reduce weight and decrease set-up time.

Stakes: A tent stake is a plastic or metal rod that's

driven into the ground to anchor a tent and rainfly. Stakes keep your tent from shifting or flying away in inclement weather. It is recommended that you stake out your tent as soon as setting it up, regardless of how pleasant the weather is at the time of arrival. You never know when a sudden wind or rainstorm might appear!

Tent Body: The main area of the tent. The body is held up by the tent poles to create the interior.

Rainfly: A piece of fabric separate from the tent body used to add protection from the wind and rain.

Product Recommendations

If you're a solo backpacker looking to keep things light and warm, the *NEMO Hornet Elite 1* tent offers 3-season coverage and weighs just over a single pound. The removable rainfly crates a small vestibule, allowing you to keep dirty and wet gear separate.

Compact in transport, yet spacious when pitched, the *REI Half Dome 2 Plus* tent is the perfect companion for backpackers who will be sharing their shelter with a friend. With ample space to stretch out, change, and store your backpack, you and your hiking partner will feel roomy in this tent.

Winter enthusiasts who enjoy camping in heavy snow and at high elevations will love *The North Face VE 25*. Able to comfortably fit three people and sporting two doors, this alpine tent will be sure to keep you cozy no matter the weather.

Backpackers that prefer to pack light and stay off the ground will enjoy tree-dwelling in the *ENO OneLink Shelter System*. The hammock has enough room for two adults and the entire system boasts a bug net and rainfly.

Families looking to stay in one tent all together will enjoy using the *MSR Papa Hubba NX 4*. With enough room to house four adults and pack down to the size of many 2-person tents, this 3-season shelter is light in the pack and perfect for those with younger kids.

To get the most up-to-date information, please visit our web article Best Backpacking Tents where you'll find the latest tent recommendations. This list is updated every year.

.

4. SLEEPING BAGS

Sleeping bags are an absolute must when hitting the trail. Having a warm container to sleep in at night is a non-negotiable creature comfort and even more importantly, a quality sleeping bag provides safety. The risk of hypothermia isn't just a danger in harsh environments, but can also be a threat in relatively warm weather too. Staying warm is one of the most critical aspects of being safe in the backcountry.

Things To Consider When Choosing A Sleeping Bag

1. Temperature

Arguably the most important consideration for a sleeping bag is its temperature rating. Understanding the rating system, and how it should be applied, is an important step in choosing the right bag for the environment you'll be sleeping in.

Temperature Ratings
When deciding on the right bag, it's always best to err on the side of caution and choose a lower temperature rating than you think you need. The lower the rating, the warmer the bag will be. In the event that you end up being too warm, it's an easy adjustment to unzip the bag and cool off. It is much harder to warm up than it is to cool down.

In order to make the most informed decision, make sure that the sleeping bag you choose is rated using one of the standardized systems: ISO (International Standards Organization) or EN (European Norm). By doing this, you'll be able to accurately compare the temperature ratings between two bags (even if one uses EN and the other uses ISO).

What Type of Sleeper Are You – Warm or Cold?

It's also important to understand that there are two temperature ratings for each bag that you should keep an eye on: Comfort Rating and Lower Limit Rating.

The Comfort Rating is the lowest allowable air temperature for cold sleepers (often thought of as women) while the Lower Limit Rating is the lowest allowable air temperature for warm sleepers (traditionally men). Because of data that shows the physiological differences in core sleeping temperature between the two binary genders, women's sleeping bags reference the Comfort Rating while men's bags rely on the Lower Limit Rating.

Temperature Rating Guidelines

Summer Season: +30°F and higher
3-Season: +15°F to +30°F
Winter Season: +15°F and lower

2. Insulation

Sleeping bags are made with two different insulation types: down and synthetic. Each type has its pros and cons.

Down

"Down" is the fluffy layer of plumage found under the exterior layer of feathers in waterfowl like geese and ducks. By far the more popular of the two, down insulation is extremely lightweight and very compressible, meaning its packed dimensions save precious room in your backpack. Although more expensive than synthetic bags, sleeping bags insulated with down are more durable and last longer, making them a great investment over the years.

An important spec to keep your eye on when choosing a down bag is how much "Fill Power" it has. The higher the number, the better the warmth to weight ratio. As you'll learn in the next section, overall sleeping bag weight is an important consideration.

Fill power is a great way to compare seemingly identical bags with the same temperature rating. For example, two 15° bags can differ by $100 depending on the fill power, but higher fill powers are more efficient.

If you can afford the price difference, a 15° bag with 850-fill power can provide as much as 10 ounces of weight savings over a 15° bag with 650-fill power! However, the benefit of choosing a bag with a lower fill power is that it allows you to get a 15° bag at an entry-level price point.

In recent years, most manufacturers have started treating down feathers with a water-resistant coating. This helps mitigate the loss of insulation efficiency if your bag gets wet. However, a soaking wet down bag will not be able to provide the amount of warmth that a wet synthetic bag will.

Synthetic

Synthetic sleeping bags offer a few advantages over down and are definitely worthy of consideration. More affordable than their down counterparts, synthetic bags will continue to keep you insulated even when wet, and will dry out much faster than a down bag. This can be a crucial difference if you'll be camping in damp or rainy climates.

Synthetic bags are also non-allergenic, meaning these are the choice for those who have sensitive allergies to bird feathers and plumage.

3. Weight

The weight of your bag is an important feature to consider, as a heavy-weight bag will take up more space and make your backpack heavier overall. While not everyone needs to be an ultralight enthusiast, weight is a crucial consideration for every piece of gear you buy. It all adds up! Sleeping bags offer some of the greatest potential weight savings.

When trimming down on weight, make sure you're comparing bags with the same temperature rating as lower degree bags require more insulation to keep you warmer. Also, keep an eye out for more efficient types of insulation that provide the same amount of desired warmth at a lower weight.

4. Shape

When it comes to bag weight vs. roominess, there are three general shapes of sleeping bags that you can choose from: mummy, semi-rectangular, and rectangular. You may also consider opting for a double sleeping bag if you and your partner prefer to stay close while you sleep.

Mummy
Best suited for backpacking trips due to their lighter weight and thoughtfully engineered design, mummy bags offer the best warmth to weight ratio of any shape. They hug you closely and come with a hood to keep your head warm.

Semi-Rectangular
These bags offer more room than mummy bags for a small tradeoff in warmth and come in a "barrel" shape.

Rectangular
Better suited for those camping for several days, rectangular bags are heavy but provide much more room to stretch out. They also do not insulate nearly as well as mummy bags, but offer the most entry-level friendly price point.

Double
An ideal choice for couples who want to share a bag, double bags offer room for two. Another choice is to pair a right-zip and left-zip bag to-

gether, giving you the option to join individual bags together to make one big bag. Rectangular bags offer this option as well.

5. Length

Traditional sleeping bags are divided into two different categories, based on the gender binary: men's and women's. All you really need to know is your height and body shape to decide which length of sleeping bag is right for you.

What are known as "men's" sleeping bags are made in Regular and Long lengths. A regular bag is usually 6' long and can fit people up to six feet tall.

A long bag measures 6' 8" and is designed for people who are taller than six feet (up to 6' 6"). The extra 8" of length in a long bag is designed to give you a little room to move about as your spine will decompress and add an inch or two to your height when you lay flat.

Some companies also include a "Short" or "Small" length of men's bag, which fits people who are shorter than 5' 6". Traditionally designed women's bags are also made for shorter individuals and they typically come in Regular and Long sizes as well.

A regular women's bag fits people up to 5' 6" and a long women's bag is good for people up to 5' 10". You can also opt for a gender-neutral bag, which will provide you with a wider selection of styles and length options. Just make sure to check the length specifications against your body height before choosing which length of bag is right for you.

6. Additional Features

Hood
Typically found on mummy and semi-rectangular bags, a sleeping bag hood helps your head trap warmth and keep your body warmer overall. When backpacking in colder climates, this is a must-have feature.

Left or Right-Zip
This is important only if you plan to join two sleeping bags together. Men's bags typically come in a left-zip while women's bags come with a right-zip. It's important to have one of each in order to properly join the two. Most brands will make matching bags for men and women (same temperature rating, insulation, etc.) that will easily pair together.

Stash Pocket
Many bags offer a convenient pocket near the chest to stash items you may need overnight such as lip balm or a headlamp.

Pillow Pocket
Some sleeping bags offer a pocket that can be stuffed with clothing to create a makeshift pillow. This is a great way to use what you already have to create comfort rather than buying an extra camp-

ing pillow.

7. Optional Accessories

Stuff Sack
Many sleeping bags come with a stuff sack that allows you to pack down the bag into a nice and tidy compartment. This is helpful when packing your multi-day pack and keeps things organized.

Compression Sack
Similar to a stuff sack, a compression sack takes things one step further by employing tension straps to compress the sleeping bag. Depending on how large the bag is, a compression sack can reduce the size of a sleeping bag into roughly the size of a gallon of milk.

Another option some compression sacks offer is waterproofing. For just a little more money, you can ensure that your sleeping bag stays 100% dry if caught in a downpour or making a water crossing on the trail.

Sleeping Bag Liner
Sleeping bag liners can be a handy addition to protecting your sleeping bag. By slipping it inside before you lay down to rest, you can prevent wear and tear on your expensive bag and keep your actual sleeping bag clean. Liners are much more durable and easier to wash than sleeping bags, so they're definitely a good option to include if you won't have access to a shower for a few days.

The best benefit of sleeping bag liners is that they can add an extra 10° – 15° degrees of insulation to your bag. Liners can extend the versatility of a 3-season bag without so you don't have to carry the extra weight of a winter bag to stay warm at night in cooler temperatures. In theory, a sleeping bag with a 30° F rating could improve to be comfortable in temperatures down to 15°F with the addition of a liner.

Techie Language Explained

Baffle: A baffle is a horizontal stripe that is sewn across a sleeping bag to hold down or synthetic material in place. A boxed baffle is the preferable style as it retains heat better. Sewn-through baffles allow heat to escape and thus do not insulate as well.

Footbox: The bottom of the bag where your feet rest. It is referred to as a footbox because sleeping bag zippers typically only go down to the ankle or mid-calf, isolating your feet into a cozy little box at the bottom of your bag.

Hook-and-loop Tab: A velcro flap that secures the zippers on the side of your sleeping bag. It's designed to prevent your bag from unzipping during the night due to movement.

Hood Drawstring: Mummy style sleeping bags often include a drawstring at the hood, allowing you to cinch the opening around your face. In extremely cold climates, the hood can be drawn almost completely around the face, allowing you to breathe easy and still remain warm.

Yoke: For sleeping bags, a yoke is a neck collar inside the bag that helps prevent warm air from escaping through the collar of the bag.

Product Recommendations

3-season backpackers needing to stay warm during early spring and late fall backpacking trips will find the *Kelty Cosmic 20* to be a trusty, go-to bag. It hits the sweet spot on all the specs making it a quality bag at a reasonable price.

Ultralight enthusiasts looking to shave down every ounce possible will love the *Therm-a-Rest Hyperion 32*. At just 16 oz. in total weight, you'll nimbly navigate your hike feeling as light as a feather and will sleep comfortably down to freezing temps.

Backpacking women looking for a fitted shape sleeping bag might consider *REI's Joule 21*. Its 700-fill-power duck down provides a temperature rating down to 21° F and an overall weight just over 2 lbs. It also comes in a Regular-Wide size to accommodate a roomier fit.

For the couple who just can't bear to be apart whilst slumbering, the *Big Agnes King Solomon 15 Double* will let you stay cozy together in temperatures down to 15° F. This bag simplifies backpacking by eliminating the need to zip together two separate bags.

Winter backpackers looking to push their limits to the extreme should consider the *REI Downtime 0*. With a lower-limit rating of 0° F, you'll be ready to take on sub-freezing temps in comfort and style.

To get the most up-to-date information, please visit our web article Best Backpacking Sleeping Bags where you'll find the latest sleeping bag recommendations. This list is updated every year.

5. SLEEPING BAG LINERS

Although not an essential item, sleeping bag liners have a host of benefits that provoke serious consideration. They protect the inside of a sleeping bag from excessive wear and tear. It's much easier and less costly to replace a bag liner than your expensive sleeping bag!

Bag liners also keep your actual sleeping bag cleaner, which in turn causes it to last longer as well. By keeping sweat, oils, and dirt out of your bag, you'll extend the life of your investment. It's also much easier to launder and clean a bag liner than a sleeping bag.

Quite possibly the most advantageous benefit of having a sleeping bag liner is the extra insulation that bag liners provide. Adding anywhere between 10° – 15° degrees of insulation, a liner can push the limits of what your sleeping bag is capable of withstanding. A sleeping bag with a lower limit rating of 30°F could potentially keep you insulated down to 15°F with the addition of a liner.

Things To Consider When Choosing A Sleeping Bag Liner

1. Materials

Cotton
As the most affordable option, cotton sleeping bag liners can add an element of comfort for those who dislike the slippery feel of a sleeping bag. Cotton, however, does not add any warmth to your bag and takes a long time to dry if it accidentally gets wet.

Fleece / Microfleece
Fleece can add a lot of warmth to a sleeping bag, making it a great choice for cold-weather backpackers looking to push their sleeping bag's tem-

perature rating to new limits. The downside is that fleece is heavy and bulky, meaning you'll be sacrificing precious space in your backpack and adding a considerable amount of weight to your shoulders.

Insulated
Insulated liners can be a pricier addition to your backpacking arsenal but can add up to 25° degrees of warmth in a super light construction. They also dry up to 50% faster than cotton, making insulated liners a great option in damp climates. Plus, insulated liners can act as their own sleeping bag in extremely warm climates, allowing you to ditch your sleeping bag entirely on hot nights and save weight in the process.

Silk
The lightest of all the options, silk liners are compact and versatile. They are breathable in warmer weather and can moderately extend the range of your sleeping bag's temperature rating in colder weather. Keep in mind that silk liners tend to fall on the pricier side of the available options.

Synthetics
Best suited for warmer and more humid environments, synthetic liners wick moisture and keep your sweat from adversely affecting your sleeping bag. They fall in the middle of the road when it comes to cost.

Techie Language Explained

Drawcord: Some bag liners that come in a mummy shape often include a drawstring/drawcord at the hood, allowing you to cinch the hood's opening. In extremely cold climates, the hood can be drawn almost completely around the face, allowing you to breathe easy and stay warm.

Hood: Typically found on mummy shaped bag liners, a hood helps your head trap warmth and keep your body warmer overall. When backpacking in colder climates, this is a must-have feature.

Mummy Shape: Bag liners with a mummy shape are designed to hug you closely and come with a hood to keep your head warm. They are usually paired with a mummy shape sleeping bag.

Stuff Sack: Many sleeping bags and liners come with a stuff sack that allows you to pack down the bag into a nice and tidy package. This is helpful when packing your multi-day pack and helps to keep things organized.

Product Recommendations

Budget-conscious backpackers looking to protect

their bag at an entry-level price point will certainly appreciate the *Cocoon Cotton Bag Liner*. This cotton liner adds a modest 5° degrees of warmth and is easy to wash after a weekend hike.

Casual campers that stay put at a campsite for a few days will benefit the most from *Sea To Summit's Fleece Liner*. The soft fleece will make your camping trip feel luxurious and provide an ample amount of extra warmth.

Winter adventurers needing to max out the temperature rating of their sleeping bag will love the *Sea To Summit Thermolite Reactor Extreme*. At just 14 oz., this liner provides up to a 25° degree increase in warmth, meaning your 15° bag can serve you in temps down to -10°F.

If you're a 4-season backpacker that enjoys versatile gear, the *Cocoon Silk Mummy Liner* will serve you well in all seasons. Adding some warmth in colder climates and letting your skin breathe in warmer ones, this liner is a top-notch choice.

Backpackers sleeping in more humid climates should take a look at the *Cocoon CoolMax Mummy Liner*. Adding 8.4° degrees of warmth, this moisture-wicking liner will keep sweat off your sleeping bag and extend its longevity.

To get the most up-to-date information, please visit our web article Best Sleeping Bag Liners where you'll find the latest bag liner recommendations. This list is updated every year

6. SLEEPING PADS

Asleeping pad may be one of the most important purchases you make for overnight camping trips along with your sleeping bag. Serving as a dual-purpose piece of gear, a sleeping pad's most important function is primarily for insulation and secondarily to provide comfort when sleeping on the ground.

There are a wide variety of different sleeping pads available today, so it's important to know how to find the one that will suit you best. In certain situations, a sleeping pad may mean the difference between a rough, cold night and staying warm, safe, and comfortable. For others, a good quality sleeping pad can stave off potential back pain and will make your next day on the trail far more enjoyable.

Things To Consider When Choosing A Sleeping Pad

1. Type

There are 3 general types of sleeping pads that each have their own pros and cons. There is no single best type of sleeping pad, just the right piece of gear for the job. As you learn about the different types of pads, keep in mind your particular preferences and needs when choosing the best fit for you.

Air Pads

Comfortable, lightweight, and compact, air pads provide some of the best bang for your buck and are offered in a range of price points. These lightweight sleeping pads inflate with air to create a soft and buoyant sleeping surface. An inflatable air pad will lift your body far enough off the ground that you'll stay warm and cozy all night long if you pair it with the appropriate sleeping bag for the season.

Summer air pads are typically less expensive than winter air pads and provide a modest amount of insulation value. Winter air pads, although pricier, provide a huge insulating advantage in extremely cold climates. Some winter pads have been known to insulate so well that backpackers actually had to unzip their sleeping bags to cool off.

Downsides to using an air pad include a higher price tag versus other types of pads, especially the more lightweight and compact they get. They are also susceptible to punctures but can be repaired in the field with ease. Lastly, air pads aren't the quietest choice and can be somewhat noisy when turning over.

Closed-Cell Foam Pads
The most basic sleeping pad you can buy is a closed-cell foam pad. Lightweight and inexpensive, these pads are highly durable and can be lashed to the outside of your backpack, freeing up precious space inside. These sleeping pads offer the best entry-level price point.

Their singular size makes them bulkier than other options and while durable, they tend to be the least comfortable option available. They are very easy to deploy as they don't require any inflation – just roll it out and you're good to go!

Closed-cell foam pads are often used in conjunction with other types of sleeping pads to add extra insulation on extremely cold nights or another layer of padding for car camping trips. One major benefit is that they can be cut to size, so if you want to carry the lightest weight possible you can trim the pad to cover only the length of your torso instead of lugging around a full body-length pad.

Self-Inflating Pads
A cross between air pads and closed-cell foam pads, self-inflating pads are a more luxurious option if you have the space to pack one and don't mind the extra weight. They tend to be wider and thicker than other options and are some of the warmest pads you can buy. Priced in the middle of the road, these pads offer a huge bump up in comfort from closed-cell foam pads, but their bulk and weight can be a downside.

Arguably the biggest advantage self-inflating pads have over air pads is their reliability. Since self-inflating pads have an open-cell foam pad within their core, they will provide some comfort and still insulate even if punctured. If you're unable to repair your self-inflating pad on the trail, you'll still have a decent night's sleep.

2. Intended Use

Consider what type of backpacking or camping you'll be doing most often. Choosing the right ground pad is as much about how you'll be using your pad as it is about your personal needs and preferences.

Backpacking
After a tough day on the trail, an air pad or self-inflating pad is going to provide the best night's sleep to help you recover for the next day's adventure. There is a wide variety of options within these two types of pads so you can choose the best intersection of price, weight, size, and warmth.

Minimalist Backpacking
Lightweight enthusiasts looking to shed ounces and keep their overall pack weight down should stick to air pads. For the extreme minimalist, consider getting a "short" pad that will trim size and weight from your knees down, saving precious ounces.

Thru-Hiking
If you're completing a through-hike of several hundred or even a few thousand miles, such as the Appalachian Trail or the Camino de Santiago, you're going to need a combination of light weight and durability. A closed-cell foam pad is your best choice, eliminating the need for repairs and saving space in your bag.

Winter Backpacking
If you'll be in extreme wintery conditions with snow and sub-freezing temperatures, the best possible choice is an air pad with a high R-value (see Techie Language Explained, below). Some manufacturers add a reflective layer that returns heat to

your body, so keep an eye out for that. It's also a good idea to bring a second pad as a backup, such as a closed-cell foam pad, in case your air pad gets punctured. It can also be doubled up to maximize your insulation power.

Car Camping
When your campsite isn't far from where you parked, a self-inflating pad will be your best bet. As the warmest and most comfortable type of pad available, weight and space shouldn't be as big of a concern.

3. Features

After deciding on what type of sleeping pad is best for you based upon your specific needs and intended use, there are a few key features that are important to keep in mind. You'll have to weigh the importance of each of these and balance them accordingly.

Insulation (R-Value)
How well a material insulates is rated by a metric called R-value, which is a measure of thermal resistance. The higher the R-value number, on a scale from 1 – 10, the better a material is able to insulate you.

Weight
Although weight is highly scrutinized by ultralight enthusiasts, all backpackers should take

it into consideration. Being strategic with your packing and keeping your multi-day pack relatively light can save you on a long hike and help you go further each day. Look for pads that come in a mummy shape or have a short version to trim down on precious ounces.

Length
This feature relates to both insulation and weight depending on what type of conditions you'll be backpacking in. If the weather is warm, consider a short sleeping pad to reduce weight. If the weather is cold, you'll need to keep your legs warm with a regular length pad (72" inches) or a long sleeping pad (78" inches) if you're above 6' 0" feet tall.

Width
Most sleeping pads have a standard width of 20". If you need something wider, a regular length pad can sometimes be found in wide sizes up to 30", or you can opt for a long sleeping pad that includes a few extra inches of width.

4. Additional Extras

Integrated Sleeping Systems
When buying your sleeping bag, check to see if there is an option to integrate a sleeping pad. Some manufacturers have a built-in sleeve that will keep your sleeping pad from sliding out from under you during the night. This can be a good

choice for restless sleepers who move a lot in the night.

If you prefer to sleep in a hammock, check to see if there is an integrated slip for a pad. Some brands, such as the ENO Double Nest hammock, offer this feature to help insulate you against cold air beneath your hammock.

Hand Pumps
When inflating an air pad, using a hand pump can make the task much simpler. Other reasons to consider using one are to prevent the buildup of moisture from your breath inside the pad. Although rare, the moisture could freeze in extremely cold environments or even cause bacteria to grow in very hot weather.

Repair Kit
If you've chosen an air pad or a self-inflating pad, a repair kit is a good way to protect your investment and help you out in a pinch while on the trail. Many pads come with a basic repair kit but it's always a good idea to have a backup or a better-quality kit that can aid in a variety of repairs.

Techie Language Explained

R-Value: The number used to determine the warmth of a sleeping pad based on its ability to resist (hence the "R") heat loss. A higher R-value equals a warmer sleeping pad. R-values are based on a scale that ranges from 1 (minimally insulated) to 11 (maximum insulation).

Stuff Sack: A compact protective pouch where you can store your sleeping pad when not in use.

High-flow Valve: In self-inflating sleeping pads, a high-flow valve is the mechanism that allows air to rush in and inflate the pad. Twist the valve again and compress the pad to force air out and deflate for travel.

Accordion-style Design: A closed-cell foam sleeping pad with an accordion-style design means that the pad folds up in a Z-like pattern instead of being rolled up. This helps it pack down in a more minimal way.

Product Recommendations

Casual backpackers and side sleepers alike will appreciate the comfort and cushion that the *REI Camp Bed Self-Inflating* Sleeping Pad provides. With an R-value of 6.8, you'll be comfortably warm without breaking the bank.

If you're an ultralight enthusiast that meticulously counts ounces and you're always looking to stay as light as possible on the trail, then the *Therm-a-Rest NeoAir UberLight* sleeping pad is one of the lightest choices possible. At just 8.8 oz. of total weight, it folds down to the size of a napkin (6" x 3.5"). It only has an R-value of 2.0, so it's not the warmest option available but it will do the trick for most seasons on the trail.

Couples looking to share the load and reduce weight between both of their packs should consider getting a double wide inflatable sleeping pad like the *Sea to Summit Comfort Deluxe*. Its surprisingly compact packed size will leave more room in your bag while allowing plenty of room for two when fully inflated.

For extreme winter backpackers looking to take on snowy climates and alpine conditions, the *Exped DownMat XP 9* offers an insulation value of R-8 to keep you toasty. Where most pads of this insulation range from 4 – 5 lbs., this pad weighs in at just under 2 lbs, saving you a lot of weight for your journey.

If you're a thru-hiker planning on backpacking hundreds or even thousands of miles in a single go, such as on the Pacific Crest Trail, consider the *Big Agnes Third Degree* foam sleeping pad. Lightweight and extremely durable, this closed-cell foam pad has two layers to help keep you warm while roughing it.

To get the most up-to-date information, please visit our web article Best Sleeping Pads for Backpacking where you'll find the latest sleeping pad recommendations. This list is updated every year.

SECTION III: COOKING

7. STOVES

A good camp stove is an essential item if you're partial to warm meals, which most people are after a long day on the trail. A hot meal while camping can be a huge benefit, providing an ample amount of energy and sustenance to keep you trekking. The ability to make a hot cup of coffee in the morning or during a particularly cold hike can also be a big morale booster.

Things To Consider When Choosing A Stove

There are quite a few options when it comes to picking out the right stove. Read on to learn about the major types of stoves, what options exist within those categories, and the benefits of each.

1. Canister Stoves

Great For: Cold Weather, High Elevation, Ultralight Hiking, Simmering Water, Ease of Use.

Canister stoves are the simplest types of stoves to operate and are usually compact and lightweight. They're a great choice for beginners who need a low-maintenance option as these stoves work by simply screwing them into a closed fuel canister that holds a combination of isobutane and propane.

These canisters cannot be refilled once they are empty, but you can pick up a new one from any outdoor gear store. An 8 oz. fuel canister can typically burn on high for 3 hours continuously, so you should be able to get some good use out of a single canister on your backpacking trip. Always make sure to bring enough fuel for your trip by calculating how many hot meals you plan to prepare and how long each meal should take to cook.

Quick and easy to light, canister stoves typically have a pressure regulator that makes it easy to adjust the amount of flame output which helps them to perform better in cold weather. However, some downsides to canister stoves are the higher cost of fuel, the need to properly recycle used canisters, and not knowing how much fuel you have left. It's best to carry a small spare canister to ensure you don't run out of fuel.

2. Integrated Canister Systems

Great For: Cold Weather, High Elevation, Large Groups, Boiling Water Rapidly, Simmering Water, Ease of Use

The newest and most efficient type of stove available, integrated canister systems can boil water in just over 1 ½ minutes. These all-in-one systems include an insulated cooking pot that securely attaches to the burner which screws into the fuel canister. Not all models are created equally however. The taller, more slender models are designed for quick-boiling but not for cooking. If you'd like to cook your meal in the pot, look for a system with a shorter and wider pot.

3. Remote Canister Stoves

Great For: Large Groups, Ultralight Hiking, Simmering Water, Ease of Use

Larger than a traditional canister stove but smaller than an integrated system, remote canister stoves offer a middle of the road option that balances weight with bells and whistles. These models keep the fuel source separate via a hose that attaches to the burner. They sit lower to the ground and provide better stability for larger pots, making them ideal for feeding large groups of people. These stoves can be used with a larger set of pots and pans as opposed to the model-specific pot included in an integrated system.

4. Liquid-Fuel Stoves

Great For: Cold Weather, High Elevation, Large Groups, Boiling & Simmering Water, International Travel

When compared to canister stoves, liquid-fuel stoves offer more options and greater flexibility but with two small downsides explained below. Liquid-fuel stoves run on white gas which is less expensive than isobutane-propane canisters and offers better performance in cold temperatures.

Versatility of fuel options on multi-fuel stoves is a huge reason for choosing these over canister stoves, especially when traveling internationally where fuel options are limited. Multi-fuel stoves can run on some, if not all, of the following:

Unleaded Auto Gasoline (Petrol)

Diesel
Kerosene
Jet Fuel

Usually lower in profile than canister stoves, liquid fuel stoves offer greater stability while cooking. You can refill and re-use the bottle that holds the fuel for a liquid-fuel stove, making them more eco-friendly than their disposable fuel counterparts. It's also much easier to determine how much fuel you have left with a separate container of liquid fuel that can be refilled when empty.

Keep in mind that because the bottles are refillable, spills are liable to happen. That's why you always want to store your liquid fuel canister at the bottom of your pack, not on top, and as far away from your food as possible. It's also advisable to store your fuel canisters on the outside of your pack in one of the side water bottle pockets to avoid any accidental leakages inside the pack. Either way, make sure the cap is screwed on tight and be aware of where the canister is at all times.

Overall, liquid fuel stoves are heavier than canister stoves and require priming before use as well as periodic maintenance, which means they might not be the best choice for total beginners or ultralight/ultrafast hikers.

Priming is the process of preparing a liquid-fuel stove for use by igniting a small amount of fuel in a cup beneath the burner and by pressurizing the system by pumping the fuel bottle. This preheats the fuel line and prepares the stove to operate properly. Make sure to read the instructions included with your stove before lighting it for the first time, and always practice using the stove at home before bringing it out into the backcountry so you're confident about how to use it safely and properly.

Another drawback of liquid-fuel stoves is that they require periodic maintenance to ensure they're working properly, such as cleaning out the fuel lines to prevent blockage and replacing any parts that may wear out. But if you take good care of this type of stove and maintain it regularly, then it can last you through all of your many adventures.

5. Alternative Fuel Stoves

Best used for thru-hikers traveling hundreds or thousands of miles, these stoves ditch traditional fuel for more creative options.

Wood-Burning Stoves
A great choice for long distance backpackers looking to simplify and not worry about refilling their fuel, a wood-burning stove relies on the small twigs and leaves found in the backcountry. Some wood-burning models have optional USB attachments to charge devices or a phone. Downsides include difficulty of use in wet conditions, areas with little to no vegetation, forests with a burn

ban in effect, and some parks where its use is prohibited above a certain elevation.

Denatured Alcohol Stoves
An ultralight backpacker's best friend, denatured alcohol stoves can weigh as little as 1 – 2 oz. and have no moving parts that would require maintenance or repair. Denatured alcohol is also inexpensive and easy to find in the U.S. However, these stoves require more fuel and take much longer to boil a pot of water than canister or liquid-fuel stoves. These stoves also require a windscreen to keep a steady flame and finding fuel outside of the U.S. can prove difficult.

Solid-Fuel Tablet Stoves
Another popular choice amongst ultralight backpackers, solid-fuel tablet stoves are inexpensive, lightweight, and extremely compact. The tablets used are easy to light, inexpensive, and can be used multiple times before completely burning up. Unfortunate consequences of using these stoves is that they are slow to boil water, can have a funky odor, and may leave a slick film on the bottom of your pots and pans.

Techie Language Explained

Piezo-Igniter: An ignition button used in camp stoves that relies on pressure to create a spark and ignite the flame.

Pressure Regulator: A small component in a stove's valve that controls the amount of fuel being fed to the fire based upon atmospheric pressure. This technology improves the performance of your stove at high-altitude and in cold temperatures while maximizing the efficiency of fuel consumption.

Priming: The first step in using a liquid-fuel stove. Priming occurs by igniting a small amount of fuel in a cup beneath the burner and by pressurizing the system by pumping the fuel bottle. This preheats the fuel line and prepares the stove to operate properly.

Windscreen: A compact screen that surrounds the flame of your stove to prevent wind from blowing out or affecting your flame.

Product Recommendations

Solo backpackers needing compact convenience will benefit greatly from *Jetboil MiniMo* Cooking System. This all-in-one system is designed to both rapidly boil and simmer water, as well as cook and eat from the main pot.

Thru-hikers looking to tackle a thousand-mile trek will be best suited with the *Solo Stove Lite* wood-burning stove. At just 9 oz. in weight, this lightweight stove ditches the need for canisters and liquid fuel, further lightening your load.

International backpackers needing a versatile stove that can utilize a variety of fuel types should strongly consider the *MSR WhisperLite International* Backpacking Stove. Able to run on white gas, kerosene, and unleaded auto gasoline, this efficient stove can offer up to 2 hours of burn time on a 20 oz. bottle of white gas.

Alpine enthusiasts that need a reliable stove above 10,000 feet should consider the *MSR Reactor Stove System* – 1.7 Liter. Able to rapidly boil water in even the most extreme environments, this award-winning stove uses less fuel to achieve outstanding results.

Families that plan to establish a basecamp for day hikes or choose to car camp will love the *Jetboil Genesis Basecamp*. Designed to function more like a kitchen, this dual-burner stove (with option to include a third burner) comes with pots and pans and can make a hearty amount of grub to feed an entire family.

To get the most up-to-date information, please visit our web article Best Backpacking Stoves where you'll find the latest stove recommendations. This list is updated every year.

8. COOKWARE

Unless you have an all-in-one integrated canister stove system, you're going to need some cookware to prepare a hot meal in the backcountry. Solo backpackers or those on weekend trips may only need a small pot, but those who plan to tackle a longer trek like a thru-hike or who are camping in a larger group may need an entire cookset.

Things To Consider When Choosing Cookware

1. Cookset or Individual Pieces

Cookset
A cookset comes with a variety of pieces, such as pots, pans, lids, and sometimes utensils, storage containers, and cups, or bowls that nest together to save room. These are a good choice for saving space in your pack and/or when cooking a larger meal for multiple people.

Individual Pieces
Solo backpackers may prefer to just buy a single piece of cookware here and there to accommodate simple needs. This can be a good choice to keep weight down, but lends itself to bulk if you end up building a whole set piece by piece because they may not fit together compactly like a prebuilt cookware set can.

2. Materials

Aluminums
Aluminum cookware is a great option for those searching for the intersection of affordability and lightweight design. A good conductor of heat, aluminum helps cook food evenly and is efficient

at simmering without burning. Although largely a durable material, aluminum does eventually break down over time with repeated exposure to acidic foods such as tomato sauce and has a tendency to dent and scratch with use.

Hard-anodized aluminum, on the other hand, offers all the benefits of traditional aluminum without any of the drawbacks. It is extremely durable but does come at a slightly higher price tag.

Stainless Steel
Not a highly recommended option, stainless steel is much heavier than aluminum and does not heat food as evenly. Although it is much more durable than aluminum, your money is better spent on hard-anodized aluminum or titanium cookware.

Titanium
The lightest option available, titanium cookware is a great choice for ultralight backpackers looking to shave as many ounces as possible off their total pack weight. Although more expensive than other options, titanium is an efficient medium that uses less heat to cook food, saving you fuel in the long run. It's also highly resistant to corroding over time.

Non-Stick Coating
Some cooksets offer non-stick coatings which makes it very easy to clean them after cooking, but these sets are less durable than other options discussed here. If chosen, be sure to use only plas-

tic utensils on the non-stick surfaces. Otherwise you'll risk accidentally scratching and degrading the non-stick surface.

Cast Iron

Intended more for car campers, a good cast iron skillet is both extremely durable and great for making delicious dinners and baking. The heavy weight of cast iron cookware disqualifies it from being a good option for backpacking though.

3. Additional Considerations

When choosing pots, keep in mind how many people you will have in your group. You'll need roughly 1 pot for every 1 – 2 people in your group, depending on what you're cooking. If you're just boiling water for dehydrated meals, then one pot for two people is fine. If you're cooking a more traditional meal with several ingredients, consider one pot per person.

Also give consideration to pot size as larger pots will accommodate more individuals and reduce the need for multiple pots and multiple burners. Your biggest pot should hold 1 pint per person in your group – so a group of 3 should have a 3-pint pot.

Lids are an optional item, but are a good idea as they help water boil and foods cook faster. Some sets include lids that can also be used as a pan, which is an important consideration for ultralight backpackers.

Lastly, be sure that your cookset includes collapsible handles or a pot lifter/gripper in order to handle hot pots and pans. Sets that use a gripper can shave down on weight rather than having an individual handle for each piece.

4. Optional Gadgets

Coffee lovers should definitely consider a French press to add to their camp kitchen. Smaller presses are made for backpackers to keep things light. For the casual car campers, a Dutch oven could be a great choice for making large, easy to prep dinners and scrumptious backcountry desserts.

Techie Language Explained

BPA-free: Bisphenol A (BPA) is a synthetic compound found in older plastics and cookware that has been linked to health concerns. Almost all cooksets today are now BPA-free and completely safe.

Carry Sack: Many cooksets include a carry sack that helps keep all the pieces together and protect them from potential scratches.

Product Recommendations

Ultralight backpackers that are looking to reduce every ounce possible will find an ultralight cooking companion in the *Snow Peak Titanium Mini Solo Cookset*. At just 6.38 oz, you get a cup that nests inside a pot with room to accommodate fuel and a stove.

Best friends and couples needing a set for two will find the *GSI Outdoors Halulite Microdualist II Cookset* to be the ultimate set for dynamic duos. With one large pot measuring in at 1.4 Liters in size, this set includes 2 bowls, 2 cups, and 2 collapsable sporks.

A backpacking crew of four such as good friends or a family should seriously consider the *Sea to Summit Alpha 2 Pot Cookset 4.2*. This set sports 4 bowls and 4 cups that nests inside 2 pots, making this 4+ person set very compact.

Car campers looking to get the most out of a cookset should look at the *GSI Outdoors Pinnacle Camper Cookset*. Including 4 plates, 4 bowls, and 4 mugs, this cookset offers a hefty 3 Liter pot with lid and a frypan.

Budget-conscious backpackers that need a quality cookset at an affordable price will benefit from *Snow Peak's Personal Cooker 3 Cookset*. Boasting two pots, a lid, a plate, a bowl, and a frypan, this set can accommodate a wide range of cooking needs.

To get the most up-to-date information, please visit our web article Best Backpacking Cookware Sets where you'll find the latest cookware recommendations. This list is updated every year.

9. UTENSILS

Personal utensils are a must have if camping overnight. A simple set of fork/spoon/knife will make eating easier and much more enjoyable.

When it comes to kitchen utensils, these are up to your discretion. Bring what you know you'll need to properly prepare and cook your meals. Putting some forethought into planning each meal you'll enjoy while on the trail will help you discern what to bring and what can be left at home in order to reduce pack weight and bulk.

What To Bring

1. Personal Utensils

Fork/Spoon/Knife
Each person in your group should have their own set of personal utensils. There are a wide variety of options and combinations when it comes to personal utensils.

Some sets include one utensil of each type and can be kept together with a lightweight keychain. Other options include "sporks" or "foons", which combine a fork and spoon into a single utensil. Some creative combo options even include a knife on the edge of the spork/foon to consolidate all three utensils into a single tool.

Personal utensils are typically made of a lightweight metal or durable plastic and can be shaped in a variety of ways to cut down on weight.

2. Cooking Items

Cooking Utensils
Depending on the complexity of the meals you'll be preparing, you may need some cooking utensils such as a spatula, serving spoon, tongs, and/or a whisk. Many of these items are made in lightweight and compact options for backpackers that

offer benefits over using your traditional in-home cooking utensils. You can also find these in combo kits or choose to purchase individual pieces and build your arsenal on an as-needed basis.

3. Additional Items

There are plenty of additional items that can be brought along to make cooking in the great outdoors easier. Many of these items are staple pieces that you'd easily find in your in-home kitchen but can easily be forgotten for you camp kitchen. Others take these standard tools and apply an inventive approach in order to make them smaller, lighter, and simpler.

Many of these items include but are not limited to: cutting boards, potato peelers, salt and pepper shakers, can openers, hard-shell egg holders, and kitchen knives. Some backpackers also get creative with their already existing backpacking tools to help them achieve the same results – multi-tools typically have a can opener and some knives can be used for chopping/peeling.

10. CLEANING ITEMS

Cleaning items are entirely an optional choice when backpacking, but they provide a level of creature comfort that can make a world of difference on the trail. Weekend backpackers will likely be fine foregoing cleaning items and just "roughing it" for a few days.

However, thru-hikers and extended trip backpackers will benefit greatly from many of the following items. The only non-negotiable item that must be brought is a trash bag/recycling bag in order to pack out what you pack in. This is in keeping with Leave No Trace Principles and will help ensure that natural areas are kept pristine.

What To Bring

1. Camp Sink / Wash Bin

When cleaning dishes for four or more backpackers, a camp sink or wash bin should be a consideration. You'll also be cleaning the pots, pans, cutting boards, and knives used to make dinner as well.

There are several options to choose from when buying a camp sink including size and weight, as well as more innovative features such as a collapsible bin. A bin that's collapsible is a non-negotiable feature for backpackers if they choose to carry a wash bin. Car campers are able to get away with more traditional and larger sized bins.

A collapsible wash bin can also be an effective tool for washing your clothes on extended multi-day hikes. Just remember to use biodegradable soap and stay 200 feet away from water sources. Dump your gray water into the earth, not rivers or streams.

2. Large Refillable Water Jug

Having water storage at your base camp is invaluable and makes cooking far easier. Being able to fill pots with water and dispense water for cleaning dishes or washing your hands makes the camp kitchen work much more functionally, just the way things would work at home.

To learn more about refillable jugs and water storage, see Chapter: Water Storage.

3. Biodegradable Soap

If you're going to be cooking on the trail, you'll also be cleaning. Leave the generic store-bought soap at home and opt for a biodegradable option. This is really a non-negotiable and is in line with following the Leave No Trace Principles.

Disposing of waste properly means doing so in a responsible manner. Traditional soaps have phosphates which can negatively impact the environment and adversely affect fragile waterways.

When using biodegradable soap to wash dishes and hands, it's important that your camp kitchen is at least 200 feet away from water sources. This will also help minimize the impacts of dirty water run-off.

4. Pot Scrubber / Sponge

These are an easy way to scrape food debris from your pots/pans and dishes without having to use your hands. A combination scrubber/scraper is an extremely useful tool, allowing you to take care of hardened food.

Another budget alternative is to buy a simple sponge with a scrubber side. You can make your sponges last longer and go further by cutting them in half. And if you really want to get creative and save money, you can always use dirt or sand as an abrasive material to scrub your especially greasy pots and pans – it works like a charm!

5. Trash Bag / Recycling Bag

Following the 7 Leave No Trace Principles is extremely important when venturing into the wilderness. Disposing of waste properly is arguably one of the most important and possibly one of the easiest ways we can minimize our impact on the environment.

Bringing a trash/recycling bag is a simple yet effective way to ensure that you can leave your campsite pristine. Remember, you must pack out what you pack in. While others may leave trash behind (whether purposefully or by accident), it is your responsibility to leave the natural places you visit cleaner than you found them.

6. Quick Dry Towel

A quick dry towel will make your cleanup simpler and more effective. Consider the weight and bulk of a roll of paper towels, not to mention the possibility of them getting wet and becoming useless.

A quick dry towel will be much more effective at helping you dry cleaned dishes and it will take up much less pack space than a roll of paper towels or a traditional cotton towel. This isn't to say that you couldn't bring a few folded paper towels in a zip-lock baggie for particularly grimy cleanup, but just remember that you must pack out what you pack in.

Quick dry towels come in many sizes for different applications. Snag a small one for kitchen cleanups and a large one for drying off after a waterfall shower.

7. Clothesline (with Clips)

A clothesline may be one of the simplest yet most effective items you can bring with you, especially if you'll be thru-hiking or backpacking for several days or weeks. Not only can you hang your quick dry towels, but you'll be able to dry your recently washed clothes quicker and more effectively too.

SECTION IV: WATER

11. WATER STORAGE

Keeping water handy and having the right gear to store water is essential when hitting the trail. Your locale, access to water, and the type of camping you'll be doing will be large factors in determining your water storage needs. Staying hydrated is not only imperative to camping and backpacking safety, but having the ability to use extra water to cook and clean also make life on the trail much easier.

Things To Consider When Choosing Water Storage

1. Types of Water Storage

Water Bottles
Water bottles are an inexpensive and easy way to store your water. Although limited in size, they do offer some advantages that make them worth considering.

Nalgene: Holding between 32 – 48 fl. oz. depending on the size, Nalgenes are lightweight and extremely durable water bottles that are made of hard plastic that is virtually impossible to break. They are transparent and include an external marking gauge that lets you measure water for cooking or keep track of how much water you've consumed. Last but not least, they are one of the least expensive options.

Vacuum Bottle: More of a luxury for campers and less practical for weight-conscious backpackers, vacuum bottles keep hot things hot and cold things cold. This is great for keeping your coffee hot on a morning hike or keeping water cool on a hot day. These bottles tend to be on the pricier end of the scale for the comfort they provide, with larger bottles costing a pretty penny. However, they offer versatility for campers such as "growler" models that can hold 64 oz. of beer and keep it cold.

Collapsible Water Bottle: Growing in popularity due to their compact size, collapsible water bottles have become larger and more durable in recent years. These handy bottles can be stashed in your bag and then filled at a water source. Some bottles can hold up to 70 fl. oz.

Hydration Reservoirs

As the most preferred method of hauling and drinking water, hydration reservoirs are able to haul anywhere between 1 – 3 liters of water. Their biggest benefit is ease of use on the trail, as they sport a drinking tube that threads through your backpack's shoulder strap. Rather than having to take off your pack to reach your water bottle, just grab the tube and take a sip.

One consideration when choosing a hydration reservoir is what size you will need relative to the types of trails you'll be backpacking. 1 Liter of water weighs roughly 2 lbs., so if you don't need to max out on water, you can save pack weight. One example would be backpacking in an area with a lot of water sources such as rivers, streams, and waterfalls. However, if you're hiking in a desert or other area with little to no water sources, then packing in as much as you can will keep you safer and better hydrated.

You also don't have to fill your entire reservoir.

If you have a 2 Liter reservoir but find yourself on a day trip, you can fill it only halfway to cut down on weight.

Large Storage Containers
Having an extra container for water storage at your basecamp is usually a good idea, especially when it comes to cooking and cleaning. Backpackers have lightweight and collapsible options while campers can load up with heftier options.

Hard-shell Water Containers: Best suited for those staying put in a single campsite, hard-shell water containers are a great choice to store water that can be used for cooking, cleaning, and drinking. Typically made of a hard plastic, these vessels can hold anywhere between 2 – 7 gallons of water.

Collapsible Water Storage: Backpackers moving camp each night will require a collapsible water storage option. Folding buckets and dromedaries are your best bet as they are lightweight when empty and can expand to hold as much as 10 Liters (2.6 Gallons).

Techie Language Explained

Bite Valve: A bite valve is a soft plastic mechanism that attaches to the end of a hydration reservoir's tube. It keeps water from dripping and allows it to flow when bitten down on.

External Capacity Gauge: A measuring system that allows you to know exactly how much water you have. These are useful in camp kitchens for cooking purposes and for keeping track of how much water you've consumed.

Product Recommendations

On-the-go backpackers needing hydration without being slowed down will get the most out of the *Osprey Hydraulics LT Reservoir* – 2.5 Liters. Able to slip into any daypack or multi-day pack with a hydration reservoir pouch, its easily accessible bite valve gives you the freedom to hydrate while hiking.

Winter backpackers needing to keep their coffee warm will be thankful for the *Hydro Flask Wide-Mouth Vacuum Water Bottle*. Able to hold 18 fl. oz., its double-walled insulation will keep things hot for 6 hours and cold for 24.

Backpacking groups of four or more will appreciate the lightweight yet sizable water storage of the *MSR Dromedary Bag* – 10 Liter. If your chosen backcountry trail offers little to no access to water for resupply, then bringing in water with this dromedary will be your best bet. The heavy-duty screw top lid allows you to hike with your reserve without leaks or splashes.

Ultralight backpackers needing a water reserve are best suited to using the *HydraPak Seeker* 2 Liter collapsible water bottle. At just 2.7 oz, you can hike in with this bag and fill it upon finding a water source.

Car campers looking to maximize their water storage will have a whopping 7 gallons with the *Reliance Aqua-Tainer*. It has an easy to use on/off spigot and a screw on vent cap for easy flow.

12. WATER TREATMENT

When camping and backpacking in the backcountry, having a way to treat the water you drink is an imperative. Staying hydrated is not only important for your body, but having access to clean drinking water is a matter of safety. Although a crystal clear water source may look completely safe to drink, it could be filled with bacteria, waste, or chemical runoff not visible to the naked eye. Having a reliable way to treat the water you find will ensure your trip won't be ruined by an upset stomach or worse.

Things To Consider When Choosing A Water Treatment System

1. Water Filters Vs. Water Purifiers

The main difference between water filters and water purifiers is what each system is able to remove from the water being treated.

Water Filter
Water filters use a physical filter to strain out impurities and microorganisms. When traveling in the U.S. and Canada, where water is already relatively safe compared to other countries, a water filter will be sufficient.

Relying on an internal cartridge, filters use pressure to force water through nano-sized holes to strain out the bacteria. This treatment system will be able to filter out parasites called "protozoan cysts" (like Cryptosporidium and Giardia lamblia) as well as bacteria (such as E. Coli, Salmonella, Campylobacter, and Shigella).

Water Purifier
If you'll be traveling outside the U.S., a water purifier is a must as it will go a step further than a filter and eliminate any potential waterborne viruses.

While some purifiers have an internal cartridge to filter bacteria as a first stage, all purifiers rely on either chemicals or ultraviolet light to destroy viruses.

2. Prefilters

Depending on what type of system you use, a prefilter may be necessary to help strain out large debris and naturally occurring sediment. Although not harmful, it is best to eliminate silt, debris, and mud by using a prefilter in order to extend the life of your microfilter. Some filters/purifiers include a prefilter; if not, it's a good idea to grab one and add it to your system. If you are using a UV purifier in murky water, you will definitely need a prefilter.

Types Of Filters And Purifiers

1. Pump Filters and Purifiers

Great For: All-Around Performance and Large Volumes of Water

One of the more basic and less expensive types of water treatment systems is the manual hand pump. These are great for shallow water sources and offer replaceable cartridges.

The element of "you get what you pay for" applies here – manual pump filters and purifiers can be tedious to use, especially after a long, exhausting day on the trail. They are also considerably bulky and weigh more than many other options in addition to requiring field maintenance.

2. Gravity Fed Filters and Purifiers

Great For: Large Volumes of Water and Ease of Use

Great for large volumes of water at sources that are deep enough to fill the bag, gravity fed water filters do all the work for you, allowing you to pitch your tent or take a break while your water gets filtered. These are great for large groups of backpackers and include a replaceable cartridge.

Although field cleaning is required, it is far less tedious compared to manual pump systems. However, when the water source is shallow or scarce, this system takes longer to use and is harder to work with.

3. Ultraviolet (UV) Purifiers

Great For: Low Maintenance, Ease of Use, and Speed of Treatment

UV light purifiers are pretty simple to use. Shaped like a wand or pen, you can fill up your water bottle, click the button, and stir. Within 60 seconds you'll have 100% clean H2O, making things a breeze. You also don't have to maintain or replace any parts if you use a UV purifier.

As quick and easy as a UV purifier is, it does require batteries and isn't good for large amounts of water. Also, if the water is particularly murky, it will need to be prefiltered before treating.

4. Bottle Filters and Purifiers

Great For: Ease of Use, Low Weight, and Speed of Treatment

Bottle filters offer easy "fill and go" simplicity, allowing you to fill up your bottle, screw the cap on, and begin drinking immediately. In this case, the water in the bottle is still dirty but is being actively treated as you sip. These are great choices for individuals on a day hike and are lightweight and inexpensive. Bottle filters also include replaceable cartridges that are inexpensive.

The limited capacity and ability to filter only when being sipped mean that bottle filters are not an ideal choice for overnight backpacking trips. Even trails that have an ample amount of water sources may only offer chances to fill up once every several miles, which means you could easily run out of water in your bottle before reaching your next source. This is not ideal as you will require more water than what your single filtering bottle can carry.

Bottle filters are also not able to provide clean water for cooking at your campsite nor does it provide clean water that may be necessary when treating wounds or administering First Aid.

5. Squeeze Filters

Great For: Ease of Use, Low Weight, and Speed of Treatment

Similar to bottle filters, squeeze filters are utilized by filling a pouch or reservoir and then squeezing the water through the filter. They also rely on replaceable cartridges that are easy to swap out and some can be used as a gravity filter without the high price tag.

The amount of water that you're able to filter is determined by the size of your reservoir but this option may not be ideal for larger groups. Field maintenance is also required for squeeze filters.

6. Straw Style Filters

Great For: Ease of Use, Low Weight, and Speed of Treatment

Great for emergencies, straw style filters are essentially a straw that allows you to sip water directly from a source. Although lightweight and offering on-demand water, these systems are pretty limited in that you may only drink when at a water source. Straws are only made to be used by one person and require field maintenance.

7. Chemical Treatment

Great For: Low Maintenance, Ease of Use, Low Weight, and Low Cost

Great for combating all types of impurities, chemical treatment is able to make clean even the dirtiest water, from bacteria to viruses. Chemical treatments utilize either iodine or chlorine via soluble pills or drops to make water safe. Lightweight, compact, and easy to use, these options are a great backup in case your main filter or purifier breaks.

Although great for treating large amounts of water with ease, these are best used as a backup because of their long wait time, anywhere between 30 minutes and 4 hours. Iodine tablets also give an odd taste to your water, but this can be improved with taste tablets.

8. Boiling

Great For: All-Around Performance, Large Volumes of Water, Low Maintenance, and Low Cost

As trusted as time, boiling water for safety is one of the most effective ways to remove pathogens and impurities in your water. This is a great backup in case your filter breaks or can be an effective primary treatment for the ultralight enthusiast. The only thing you need is an extra fuel canister for your stove.

As reliable as boiling is, it is best used as a backup plan as it takes a considerable amount of time for the water to boil and then cool. Also, depending on the size of your pot, the amount of water you'll have is limited.

Note: When treating water this way, let boil for 1 minute after reaching the boiling point. If you're above 6,500 feet, let boil for 3 minutes for maximum effectiveness.

Techie Language Explained

Flow Rate: How fast a water treatment system is able to filter water. Flow rate is typically measured in liters per minute.

Activated Carbon or Carbon Filter: A carbon filter is an extra stage in the filtration process that improves the taste of water.

Quick-connect Fitting: An optional accessory that is useful for attaching a water filter's output hose to a hydration reservoir. The result is clean water pumped straight into your water storage container.

Sediment Trap: Some filtration systems include a sediment trap to prevent fine grain sediment from clogging the filter, lending it to less maintenance and a longer filter life.

Product Recommendations

Large groups of backpackers (4 or more people) need to filter a lot of water at a decent speed for both hydration and cooking. The *Katadyn Base Camp Pro 10L* is best for larger groups as it holds a whopping 2.6 gallons of water and can filter it all in just 5 minutes.

International backpackers needing to protect against some of the most potentially dangerous water will be best aided by the *SteriPEN Classic 3* Purifier with Prefilter. Equipped with a prefilter to handle murky water, this pen can completely purify 32 oz. of water in just 90 seconds.

Casual hikers going on day hikes don't need a full water treatment system, just a trusty bottle to keep on hand when thirst arises. For casual day hikes with a reliable water source, the *LifeStraw Go* Filter Bottle 22 oz. is a perfect match.

Backpackers on a budget that need water filtration should consider the *Sawyer Squeeze* Water Filter System. This package deal gives you two 32 oz. pouches that can be stashed and stored easily.

Ultralight backpackers looking for a low-weight, low-maintenance option will love the *MSR TrailShot Pocket Sized* Water Filter. At just 5.2 oz., you can drink on the go (similar to a straw) or attach it to your hydration reservoir to replenish your water without even having to take your pack off.

To get the most up-to-date information, please visit our web articles Best Backpacking Water Filters and Best Backpacking Water Purifiers where you'll find the latest water treatment recommendations. This list is updated every year.

SECTION V: NAVIGATION

13. COMPASSES

A map and compass are two of the most essential items you need when going into the wilderness. Not only will these two trusty items help you navigate where you're going, they can also help you better understand the lay of the land and allow you to plot a new course last minute in case danger arises (such as a thunderstorm, forest fire, flooding, bear sighting, etc.).

Things To Consider When Choosing A Compass

Knowing how to properly choose, use, and calibrate a compass is an essential skill when backpacking in remote areas. Although a map alone can sometimes be sufficient for your needs, a compass is an invaluable tool that can help you triangulate your current position and plot a course.

As with any piece of gear, there are basic and more advanced features that can be found on a variety of models. However, a compass is one of the few items where you will need as many of the advanced features as possible.

While advanced features increase the price of the compass, they also vastly increase the quality. The more advanced features you have (and know how to use), the less likely you are to take an inaccurate reading which translates into a lower potential for getting lost.

1. Baseplate

The baseplate is the canvas upon which the compass sits. It has many useful features including a ruler (to measure distances on the map), navigational markings, and a straightedge to help you take a bearing (see definition below).

2. Direction-Of-Travel Arrow

When taking or following a bearing, this arrow indicates what direction to point the compass in. It is printed on the baseplate of the compass.

3. Rotating Bezel

This is the ring that surrounds the magnetized needle. It has tick marks counting to 360° degrees and is designed to help you take a bearing.

4. Index Line

Not to be confused with the index lines found on a topographic map, the index line on a compass is located above the bezel on the baseplate. The index line is the marker where you read your bearing.

5. Magnetized Needle

The key ingredient of any compass, the needle has a red portion that is magnetized to point to magnetic north.

6. Orienting Arrow

The orienting arrow is found on the glass that houses the needle. It is an outline that perfectly fits the needle and can be adjusted from its home position using the rotating bezel. Its purpose is to help orient the bezel.

7. Orienting Lines

These parallel lines are also positioned within the bezel (and rotate with the bezel). When aligned with the North-South lines on your map, these lines correctly point your orienting arrow to North.

8. Clinometer

This tool helps you measure the vertical grade of a slope (how steep it is).

9. Declination Adjustment

Depending on where you are in the world, there is a variable discrepancy between true north and magnetic north. "Declination" is the difference between these two directions and is measured in degrees. A compass that features adjustable declination allows you to "synchronize" your compass with where you are in order to take a precise bearing and properly navigate.

This is a non-negotiable feature and is imperative to have on any compass you intend to use for successful navigation.

10. Global Needle

A compass with a global needle is able to work worldwide. If it doesn't have this feature, then it will be specific to and only work in either the Northern or Southern Hemisphere.

11. Sighting Mirror

When following a bearing over a long distance, a sighting mirror will help you follow that bearing more precisely and reduce the possibility of getting off course. It can also double as a signaling device in an emergency situation.

Additional Considerations

Since your compass relies on magnetism, be mindful of where you use and store it. When taking a reading, vehicles and large pieces of metal such as signs or railroads can throw off your reading. When storing your compass, keep it away from magnets (such as those found on hydration reservoir bite valves) and cell phones, as these can demagnetize your compass.

Techie Language Explained

Bearing: A measurement of the horizontal angle

between true north and another location, or between two locations on a map. It is measured in degrees and changes based upon your current location.

Declination: A measurement of the distance between true north and magnetic north. It is measured in degrees and changes based upon your current location.

Product Recommendations

Ultralight backpackers that need a reliable compass at its very lightest will do well to use the *Brunton TruArc 3*. At just 1.1 oz., this is the lightest compass available and foregoes the need for keeping track of a declination tool.

Gadget junkies wanting every possible feature in a compass should consider the *Suunto MC-2G Navigator*. This advanced compass sports a sight-notch mirror to take incredibly accurate readings that can be doubled as a signal mirror in case of emergency.

Budget backpackers looking for an accurate and high-quality compass at an affordable price should consider the *Brunton 8010 Glow*. At just $30, you'll be able to effectively navigate at an entry level price point and use the glow feature to read a bearing in low light.

Thru-hikers needing a reliable and highly rated compass should depend on the *Suunto M-3 D Leader* Compass. Proven time and again to accurately assist in navigation, this compass is an industry standard.

Multi-discipline backpackers that backpack and paddle on the same trip (such as packrafting) will benefit the most from the *Suunto MCB Amphibian* Compass. This compass floats in water and has a built-in distress whistle for those needing to navigate on the river.

To get the most up-to-date information, please visit our web article Best Hiking Compasses where you'll find the latest compass recommendations. This list is updated every year.

14. GPS DEVICES

GPS has become a fairly ubiquitous piece of technology in the last decade and is found in an increasing number of devices, from watches to phones and everything in between. Although their implementation in smartphones is nothing short of revolutionary, dedicated GPS units still offer a large advantage and feature a variety of benefits.

Compared to smartphones, traditional GPS devices are extremely durable (the screen won't crack) and water resistant, they have better reception in remote areas, and they use replaceable batteries – the need to recharge isn't dire when you can bring along an extra set of batteries!

Although it isn't necessarily a "need", a GPS device can offer invaluable information as you navigate on the trail. You can see what path you've taken, map out where you'd like to go, and see where you currently are.

Why Use A Gps Device?

Although the range of GPS units is vast with some offering limited capabilities and others providing a host of advanced features, all GPS units do the following four basic things:

Tell You Where You Are
Not only will the GPS display where you are on a map, it will give you the coordinates of your precise location.

Record Where You've Been
Tracking is a feature that can be turned on or off. When turned on, the GPS will periodically pin your location to the map, thus showing you the path you've taken.

Help You Navigate to a Destination
Whether you've pre-loaded your destination by entering in coordinates or chosen your final des-

tination on the map while on the trail, a GPS will help you navigate where you need to go.

Give You Trip Info
GPS devices will also record data such as how far you've traveled, how long it took, your average speed, how much elevation you've gained, etc.

Things To Consider When Choosing A Gps System

This chapter solely covers GPS units for hiking and the outdoors. It does not cover fitness trackers, smartphones, smartphone apps, watches, or smart watches.

For information on GPS-enabled communication devices such as satellite messengers, see Chapter: Communication Devices.

Additionally, GPS devices are not a replacement for a map and compass but rather they are a high-tech supporting device. To learn more about analog navigation, see Chapter: Maps and Compasses.

1. Size

The size of a GPS unit is usually determined by how large the screen is. The bigger the screen, the bigger the GPS. Consider your particular needs. If you need a smaller device or don't mind a more compact screen, then you'll be able to keep your weight down. Additionally, choosing a unit with a dedicated touchscreen will also keep the size and weight down.

2. Interface

While touchscreens offer the advantage of having a potentially more compact device, consider what type of weather you will be using the GPS in the most. If you'll be in relatively moderate to warm weather, then a touchscreen is a good option and can even allow for a larger screen. However, if you'll be in wintery/snowy climates, a touchscreen will be difficult to use with gloves and a traditional interface with physical buttons will serve you better.

3. Advanced Features

GPS units don't need to have fancy bells and whistles to be effective and provide you with top notch reliability. But for those who appreciate higher end models, there are a variety of advanced features that can expand your capabilities.

Barometer/Altimeter

A built-in altimeter will give you a more accurate reading for your altitude as opposed to the GPS altitude reading given by the satellite. Additionally, a barometer is able to measure the atmospheric pressure and provide weather data, a handy tool for keeping track of ever-changing weather conditions.

Electronic Compass

This seemingly small feature is actually useful. While all GPS units are able to tell you what direction you're headed by tracking movement, an electronic compass will tell you which direction you're facing while standing still.

Preloaded Maps

Depending on the model you choose, the preloaded maps on your device can range from simplistic to extremely detailed topographic maps.

Third-Party Maps and Software

Most manufacturers offer additional maps that can be downloaded from their website, sometimes charging a fee. This is the simplest way to add more specific maps to your device. However, there are a variety of resources online that provide the same types of maps for free, you just have to do a little searching.

Memory and Data

Most GPS devices have the option to expand their memory capacity by upgrading the microSD card. If you need to store multiple detailed maps, then upgrading your memory will be a necessity.

However, most units have enough memory out of the box to store a few maps (and waypoint tracks) for a backpacking trip or two. If you fill up your memory card, you can easily delete old maps to create more room.

Two-Way Radio
Some GPS devices have a two-way radio built in, reducing your overall weight by combining two devices in one. One of the unique features of these devices is peer-to-peer positioning, which allows your friends to see your coordinates. For more information on two-way radios, refer to Chapter: Communication Devices.

Wireless Data Transfer
Provided you and a friend are using the same brand of GPS, you can wirelessly transfer data to each other's device such as maps, routes, waypoints, and more.

Techie Language Explained

GLONASS: Also known as GLObal NAvigation Satellite System, GLONASS' are Russian satellites that also support GPS devices. Although U.S.-based GPS satellites have better positional accuracy, GLONASS satellites operate on different orbits that make them more effective at higher latitudes (far north and far south).

IPX: A measure of water-resistance / waterproofing; the higher the number, the better it resists water.

IPX 1 – 4: Water resistant to small drops of water and light splashes

IPX 5 – 6: Water resistant to large and powerful blasts and sprays of water

IPX 7: Fully waterproof up to 3 feet (1 meter)

IPX 8: Fully waterproof in water over 3 feet (1 meter)

Topographic Maps: A topographic map shows the features of the earth, including but not limited to: roads, trails, bodies of water, buildings, boundaries, mountains, vegetation type, terrain, and slope. These are incredibly useful for planning a route as they can show you the limits, extremes, and possibilities for your path.

Product Recommendations

Thru-hikers looking for a solid GPS with a touchscreen interface might like the *Garmin eTrex 32x*. At just 5 oz., it's light enough to tackle even the most difficult trails and sports an IPX-7 waterproof rating.

Budget backpackers needing a reliable GPS at an entry-level price point will get the best bang for their buck with the *Garmin eTrex 20x*. At just under $200, this affordable unit can save up to 200 routes and 2,000 waypoints.

Winter backpackers needing a traditional interface with physical buttons will love the *Garmin GPSMAP 64sx*. It comes with preloaded topo-maps and can connect to other devices via Bluetooth.

Gadget junkies who like having devices that sport every bell and whistle will appreciate the *Garmin Oregon 750t*. It sports a vibrant color display, has 8 GB of internal memory and includes an 8-megapixel camera to take pictures of your waypoints.

Ultralight backpackers needing a GPS at its very lightest may find the *Garmin Foretrex 601* to be their best choice. At just 3.1 oz. including batteries, this GPS opts for a paired down display that still gives loads of trail info.

To get the most up-to-date information, please visit our web article Best GPS for Hiking where you'll find the latest GPS device recommendations. This list is updated every year.

15. WATCHES

A good hiking watch is quite a boon when exploring the backcountry and can provide a lot of useful information at both a moment's notice and well after you've left the trail. Sporting a host of technological features that can provide insightful data, hiking watches are a luxury on the trail. Considering the price point and lack of absolute necessity, these accessories are best left as one of the last pieces you add to your arsenal.

Things To Consider When Choosing A Hiking Watch

1. Features

Altimeter/Barometer

An altimeter is a handy tool to have attached to your wrist, especially if your GPS unit doesn't have one built in. It's able to offer a more accurate reading of your altitude than a satellite-based GPS and isn't prone to signals being blocked if you find yourself in a slot canyon or under dense tree cover.

Additionally, a barometer measures the pressure of the atmosphere and provides information on local weather. This is an exceptionally useful tool for keeping track of weather conditions that can change at a moment's notice.

Compass

Although not a replacement for a traditional compass, a compass built into your watch can provide you with a convenient point of reference. Make sure the watch has a 3D compass instead of a 2D one, since it will be much more accurate.

GPS/Wi-Fi Connectivity

Depending on the power and complexity of the built-in GPS, some watches have the potential to replace your GPS device for a more compact, wearable piece of tech. Watches with basic GPS offer altitude and weather data while more advanced models can give you turn by turn navigation assistance.

Most watches that have GPS also include Wi-Fi connectivity, allowing you to sync real-time data with your phone and act as a fitness tracker (recording steps, altitude, distance, pace, etc.).

Thermometer
This is a feature that has proven to be less than reliable when the watch is worn on your wrist, since body heat throws off the readings. However, if attached to your pack then the thermometer is usually pretty accurate. A thermometer can provide you with an understanding of how cool it's going to get at night or how hot it is during the day while you're hiking, which can be handy when you're on the trail and trying to decide what to wear in the morning or how many layers to sleep in.

Water Resistance
Most, if not all, hiking watches are water resistant to some degree. Check the rating to see just how resistance it is, since some watches are able to be fully submerged for swimming and other water activities.

Techie Language Explained

GLONASS: Also known as GLObal NAvigation Satellite System, GLONASS are Russian satellites that also support GPS devices. Although U.S.-based GPS satellites have better positional accuracy, GLONASS satellites operate on different orbits that make them more effective at higher latitudes (far north and far south).

IPX: A measure of water-resistance / waterproofing; the higher the number, the better it resists water.

IPX 1 – 4: Water resistant to small drops of water and light splashes

IPX 5 – 6: Water resistant to large and powerful blasts and sprays of water

IPX 7: Fully waterproof up to 3 feet (1 meter)

IPX 8: Fully waterproof in water over 3 feet (1 meter)

VO2 Max: A measure of your body's ability to perform efficiently during aerobic exercise. The higher the number, the more effectively your body can carry and use oxygen during exercise.

Product Recommendations

Budget conscious backpackers desiring GPS watch

may find the *Garmin Forerunner 45* GPS Watch to be their best option. With an entry-level price point for GPS watches, this watch is water resistant up to 50 meters and includes a fitness tracker among a host of other features.

Gear junkies looking for a precise altimeter watch will love the *Suunto Core* Watch. Relying on a pressure based digital sensor, this watch also sports a barometer that will give weather reports and show weather data from the previous 3 – 6 hours.

Serious backpackers looking to get the best bang for their buck watch with a wide array of features should consider grabbing the *Garmin Instinct GPS Watch*. Smartphone compatible to relay data wirelessly, this watch also has a very accurate 3-axis (3D) compass, a heart rate monitor, and can connect to GLONASS as well as GPS.

Multisport hikers that also find themselves on the coast a lot should consider the *Casio Pro Trek PRW2500-1* Multifunction Watch. With equal instruments for hiking and watersports, this altimeter watch will track the local tides to help you plan your excursions and is water resistant down to 200 meters.

Fitness addicts who love to train for their outdoor adventures with intense hikes and mountain running will find the *Garmin Fenix 5X* GPS Watch to have all the right features. Able to track key performance data such as your VO2 Max and recovery time, this watch can also be paired with a heart rate chest strap to capture the most accurate readings and record additional data.

To get the most up-to-date information, please visit our web article Best Hiking Watches where you'll find the latest hiking watch recommendations. This list is updated every year.

SECTION VI: ACCESSORIES

16. TREKKING POLES

Trekking poles are an optional accessory but can be quite useful in many situations. First and foremost, they provide stability when traveling across difficult terrain and support your load when making treacherous river crossings. They can also provide extra support for guy lines when setting up a tent and can even replace some tent poles, allowing for multi-use and less equipment.

Perhaps their most effective function is a little-known fact: when descending a steep trail, using trekking poles reduces the pressure on one's knees by up to 30%. This means less wear and tear on your body, thus allowing you to minimize recovery time and travel further each day.

Things To Consider When Choosing Trekking Poles

1. Types of Trekking Poles

Trekking Poles vs. Hiking Staff
Trekking poles come in pairs and are used to help navigate difficult terrain. They are best suited for hiking and backpacking as they help ease the load being carried.

A hiking staff or stick is better used for day hikes when you won't be carrying several pounds on your back. Although they can help for rugged trails, their strength lies in more casual trails.

2. Features

Trekking poles can include a variety of features that allow for customization and can enhance your on-trail experience.

Adjustable
Most poles can have their length adjusted to be anywhere from 24" to 55" inches long. The option of adjustable length is one of the most useful

features you can find for compact storage of trekking poles. Being able to shorten your pole length is also useful when going uphill or if you plan on letting your shorter or taller friend borrow your poles for a hike.

Fixed-Length
Fixed-length poles are a great choice if you don't require an adjustable length and are an ideal choice for ultralight backpackers. Less parts and mechanisms mean less weight.

Note: Fixed length poles still shorten for stowing, they just don't allow the extended length to be adjusted.

Foldable
Trekking poles that fold down are also a great choice for ultralight enthusiasts and are a great packable option as opposed to fixed-length poles. They pull apart and snap into place much in the same way that tent poles fold up.

Shock-Absorbing Poles
Best suited for hikers and backpackers with hip, knee, or ankle trouble, these spring-loaded poles help take even more force off your sensitive joints than standard poles. The spring-loaded feature can usually be turned off when ascending.

Standard Poles
Standard poles are not only less expensive than shock-absorbing poles, they are also lighter in weight. Standard trekking poles are still a great

choice for relieving pressure and force from the knees and other joints, though they won't be as helpful as shock-absorbing poles.

Ultralight Poles
Weighing less than 8 oz. per pole, ultralight trekking poles offer easier packability and less effort, making them feel almost like an extension of yourself. Less fatigue means more energy to tackle tomorrow's trek.

Camera Mount
Some trekking poles offer an option to mount your camera on or near the handle, letting you double your pole as a monopod.

3. Length

When determining your choice of poles, your elbows should rest at a 90° angle when holding the poles on a flat surface. The length of your poles will be determined based upon whether you've chosen fixed-length or adjustable poles.

Fixed-Length Poles
Backpackers preferring a fixed-length pole should refer to the chart below to determine their best fit.

The suggested pole lengths for your height, are the following.

Up to 5' feet tall: 100 cm (39 in.)

5' 1" – 5' 7": 110 cm (43 in.)
5' 8" – 5' 11": 120 cm (47 in.)
Over 6' feet tall: 130 cm (51 in.)

Adjustable Poles

Most adjustable length poles will be suitable for those who are 6' ft tall and under. For people over 6' ft tall, you'll want poles that can reach at least 130 cm (51" in.) in length.

4. Locking Mechanisms

All trekking poles use a locking mechanism that allows them to expand for use and collapse when stowed, even fixed-length poles. Adjustable poles also use the locking mechanism to help dial in the right length. Different sets of poles use different mechanisms, each of which has their advantages.

External Lever Lock

Usually found on adjustable length poles, this quick-clamp type mechanism is easily adjustable.

Push-Button Lock

Most common on fixed-length trekking poles, push button locks pop into place when the pole is fully extended. Just push the button back in and twist to collapse.

Twist Lock

Stronger than other locking mechanisms, twist locks simply twist in one direction to loosen for adjusting the length and then twist in the other direction to tighten.

Combination Lock
Some trekking poles use more than one method to achieve their desired length, leading them to combine two different mechanisms.

5. Shaft Materials

The materials used in the shaft determine the overall weight of the pole, lending itself to be an important spec to keep in mind.

Aluminum
Highly durable and typically offered at an entry-level price point, aluminum trekking poles are unlikely to break and weigh anywhere from 18 to 22 oz.

Composite
Typically using a carbon blend or made entirely from carbon-fiber, composite trekking poles are very light and come with an increased price tag. They weigh anywhere between 12 to 16 oz., a huge upside for ultralight enthusiasts. However, if used in extreme conditions, there is a potential for these poles to break.

6. Trekking Pole Grips

The grip of a trekking pole is where you place your hand while in use. Grips are offered in a variety of materials, so it's important to find the one that suits you best. Some poles have their grips set to a 15° angle to help keep your hands and wrists in an ergonomic position, reducing fatigue from holding the poles for many hours at a time.

Cork
Best for warm weather use, cork grips resist palm sweat allowing you to keep a secure grip no matter what. Cork is also good at reducing vibrations while trekking.

Foam
Also good for resisting sweat, foam is a softer grip material that some people prefer.

Rubber
Best suited to cold weather use, rubber grips help insulate your hands and reduce vibrations from sweating. These are not recommended for summer use as they will cause your hands to sweat and possibly blister.

7. Additional Considerations

Wrist Straps
Wrist straps help support your hands and wrists while using trekking poles and allow you to keep a loose, ergonomic grip. Most straps are adjustable, allowing you to dial in the right fit.

To use them correctly, insert your hand through the bottom of the strap and then pull down and grab the pole grip.

Baskets

A trekking pole basket is a disc that attaches to the end of the pole, roughly an inch from the tip. These prevent your pole from digging too deep into the terrain and are removable when not needed. They can also be swapped out for larger baskets when trekking in snow or mud.

Pole Tips

Your pole's tips are likely either steel or carbide and help provide traction. They can be swapped for rubber tips if you're trekking on a hard surface such as asphalt or dry, compact ground.

Techie Language Explained

EVA Foam: Stands for ethylene-vinyl acetate material, which offers both padding and shock absorption.

Polyethylene: A plastic chemical compound used as a coating to reinforce and provide additional strength to a material.

Kevlar: A woven fabric that is incredibly strong and highly durable. Kevlar is the fabric used to stop bullets in bullet-proof vests.

Product Recommendations

Casual hikers that hit the trail a few times each year will be best suited with the *REI Traverse Power Lock Cork*. With an entry-level price point and comfy cork grips, these poles will give you year-round use for whatever conditions you find yourself in.

Long distance backpackers doing either weekend trips or thru-hikes will appreciate the shock absorbing power of the *Leki Micro Vario Carbon AS*. Able to reduce impacts by as much as 40%, these poles will save your joints and ligaments for tomorrow's push.

Women looking for a lightweight and highly durable set of poles should consider the *Leki Cressida Cor-Tec – Women's*. The smaller grips and more compact design all lend them to easy stowing when not in use.

Ultralight enthusiasts that desire the lightest gear will love the *REI Flash Carbon*. At just 7.4 oz per pole, every aspect has been trimmed down, including minimally styled baskets that can be removed for even lighter trekking.

Backpacking photographers needing a dual-purpose piece of gear should consider the *Mountain Trekker FX Lite Monopod*. This hiking staff doubles as a monopod to help you capture stable and crisp photographs of your favorite backcountry scenery.

To get the most up-to-date information, please visit our web article Best Hiking Poles where you'll find the latest trekking pole recommendations. This list is updated every year.

17. HEADLAMPS

A trusty headlamp is an essential accessory when backpacking and much easier to handle than a flashlight as it offers hands-free assistance. As the sun sets and you're setting up camp, having a reliable source of light to pitch your tent and cook is a must have. Midnight bathroom breaks alone are reason enough to have one on hand (or head).

Headlamps are also helpful for hikers when navigating back to the trailhead. Sometimes the sun sets sooner than we expect and having a headlamp can make your last few miles much more manageable.

Things To Consider When Choosing A Headlamp

1. Comparing Specs

When comparing two or more headlamps, there are several specs that can be matched against each other. Read below to take these considerations into account.

Beam Type
The beam type of a headlamp is either flood, spot, or a combination of both. Flood beam types are best for performing tasks close to the source of light and do not put out a lot of light. Spot beam types offer a more concentrated output and are best for navigating a dark trail, letting you see much further in front of you.

Output
The output of a headlamp is measured in Lumens, or the total amount of light output in any and all directions. Generally speaking, the higher the number of Lumens, the brighter the light (and the more energy consumed to make that light brighter). Although there are some exceptions to this where some manufacturers make more effi-

cient headlamps, this is a pretty reliable way of comparing two headlamps.

Distance
Distance is just as important a consideration as Lumens to the extent that it tells you how far the light from the headlamp will reach, rather than just how bright it is. The distance of a headlamp is measured in meters.

Runtime
The runtime of a headlamp is how long your headlamp will be able to produce light on a single charge and also plays an important factor when comparing two models.

Weight
Most headlamps are pretty similar in size and weight, most weighing under 7 oz. Ultralight backpackers may be more interested in saving .5 oz here, but overall there aren't large savings in weight.

2. Brightness / Light Modes

Most headlamps are equipped with varying levels of brightness and some even include different modes of how the light is transmitted.

Low
This is the most commonly used setting and uses the least amount of battery. It's great for using around the campsite and when walking on easy

trails.

Mid
Many models of headlamp offer either one or several varying levels that allows you to adjust the brightness to your desired output.

High
The maximum light level can be useful for especially treacherous paths.

Boost/Zoom
A rare option offered on select models, this feature allows a very intense burst of light for a short period of time to get a better look at something specific. This feature is very battery-intensive and should be used sparingly.

Strobe/Flash
Used primarily for emergency situations, the strobe/flash is important in helping identifying individuals in distress.

Low Light
Some headlamps include a red light that is extremely useful in the middle of the night when you may need to take a bathroom break or locate something in your backpack. Red light is the lowest visible light on the spectrum and allows your eyes to adjust the easiest. It also keeps the bugs away!

3. Additional Considerations

Batteries

Lithium batteries are a great choice for cold weather usage when compared against alkaline batteries. However, alkaline batteries do an excellent job at holding their charge and can be a good backup to have. Rechargeable batteries are also good at handling cold weather conditions but can lose charge when used infrequently.

On/Off Switch

Each manufacturer offers a unique on/off switch that determines how a headlamp cycles through its different modes. Some headlamps include an adjustable knob to do this while others have a simple button.

Tilt

Many headlamps include a tilt option, allowing you to position the light where it needs to be.

Regulated Output

Some headlamps begin to dim as the batteries drain and die. This can be annoying as it affects the output of your headlamp. However, some people see this feature as beneficial because it allows time (and light) to find and replace the batteries.

Regulated output is a unique feature that allows your headlamp to continue producing light at full power, even as the batteries dim. The downside to this feature is that once the batteries are dead, your headlamp goes out unexpectedly without warning.

Water Resistance

Most headlamps are water resistant and able to withstand rain and snow. Rare models are waterproof at shallow depths.

Techie Language Explained

IPX: A measure of water-resistance / waterproofing; the higher the number, the better it resists water.

IPX 1 – 4: Water resistant to small drops of water and light splashes

IPX 5 – 6: Water resistant to large and powerful blasts and sprays of water

IPX 7: Fully waterproof up to 3 feet (1 meter)

IPX 8: Fully waterproof in water over 3 feet (1 meter)

Brightness Memory: Headlamps with a brightness memory allow you to turn the headlamp on and off at the desired/chosen brightness level without having to readjust it each time it's turned on.

Product Recommendations

Serious backpackers hitting the trail once or twice each month will love the *Black Diamond Spot 325*. Compact and durable, this headlamp produces a whopping 325 lumens of light and can work in up to 3 feet of water for 30 minutes.

Casual hikers that go hiking a few times per year should keep the *Black Diamond Astro 175* handy for when the sun may set before making it back to the parking lot. It produces a respectable 175 lumens of light while offering an entry-level price point.

Ultralight enthusiasts that have a need to squeeze every last ounce out of their gear should opt for the *BioLite 330*. At just 2.43 oz, this rechargeable headlamp offers up to 40 hours of runtime on a single charge.

For the rugged outdoorsman who finds themselves needing highly durable gear, the *Petzl Pixa 3 Pro* is a solid choice for a luminary companion. It can be mounted to helmets and is shock resistant.

Backpackers wanting to mount their headlamp in creative places will enjoy the *Petzl Zipka*. Its unique retractable cord allows it to be mounted to your wrist, the handlebars of a mountain bike, or even your backpack.

To get the most up-to-date information, please visit our web article Best Hiking Headlamps where you'll find the latest headlamp recommendations. This list is updated every year.

18. BINOCULARS

Binoculars are a completely optional accessory, but they can be a very useful tool for spotting your next destination on the trail or for getting a closer look at wildlife. Keeping a healthy distance while observing a brown bear or an eagle in its natural habitat is made possible with a handy pair of binoculars.

Things To Consider When Choosing A

Pair Of Binoculars

1. Size

Full-Size
Common Specs: 8 x 42, 10 x 50

Best For: Tracking Wildlife, Serious Birdwatching, Car Camping, and Use on Boats

A great choice for car campers who want a great view of wildlife, full-size binoculars have a wide field of view that makes it easy to enjoy birds and other animals from a distance. Full-size binoculars are also great in low light environments, such as at dawn or sunset, due to their ability to allow more light through the lenses. As great as full-size binoculars are, they are too heavy and too bulky for backpacking.

Mid-Size
Common Specs: 7 x 35, 10 x 32

Best For: Viewing Wildlife, Day Hikes, and Sports

A step down from full-size, mid-sized binoculars are able to strike a balance between size/weight and their overall power. They are still too heavy for backpacking, but can be a great choice for day hikes.

Compact
Common Specs: 8 x 25, 10 x 25

Best For: Backpacking and Casual Outdoor Activities

The smallest and lightest option available, compact binoculars are great choice for backpackers intent on viewing wildlife and for those who need a casual pair of binoculars.

2. Primary Specs

These major specs will help you better understand binoculars and how to compare two pairs that look identical.

The most important specs to understand are the first two numbers listed (for example: 10 x 32). The first number refers to the magnification power while the second number describes the objective lens diameter.

Magnification Power
Example Specs: 10 x 32

Binoculars with a magnification power of 10 means that objects in your field of view will appear 10x closer than they would to the naked eye. The higher the magnification power, the closer objects will appear. Conversely, higher magnification power can bring objects much further away into view.

It's important to note that these higher magnification numbers also amplify the steadiness of your hands, so shakiness will appear much more exaggerated.

Objective Lens Diameter
Example Specs: 10 x 32

The "objective lens" on a pair of binoculars is the set of lenses that are closest to the object being viewed (i.e. not the lenses that you peer through). The second number refers to the size of these objective lenses in millimeters. Using the example above, a pair of binoculars with the specs 10 x 32 have objective lenses with a 32 mm diameter.

When comparing two binoculars that have the same magnification power, the pair that has a higher second number (objective lens diameter) will allow more light to pass through its lenses, thus allowing them to perform better in low light.

3. Additional Specs

Exit Pupil
Example Specs: 10 x 32, 10 x 50

Exit pupil determines how well an object can be viewed in low light or how bright an object will appear. The higher the exit pupil number, the better a pair of binoculars will be able to handle low light.

Exit pupil is determined by dividing Objective Lens Diameter by the Magnification Power, or by dividing the second number by the first number. Using the example specs above, a pair of binoculars with specs of 10 x 32 will have an Exit Pupil number of 3.2 (32/10), whereas the pair with higher objective lens diameter, 10 x 50, will have an Exit Pupil number of 5 (50/10).

Generally speaking, binoculars with an Exit Pupil number of 5 or higher are great for use in low-light such as dawn or dusk. Models with an Exit Pupil number of less than 5 are best used for daytime viewing.

Relative Brightness
Relative brightness is related to a binoculars' exit pupil number in that it measures how bright an object will appear when viewed. The higher the number, the brighter the object will appear, which is useful in low light.

To find the relative brightness of a pair of binoculars, multiply the exit pupil number by itself (in other words, square the value of the exit pupil). Using the examples above, a pair of binoculars with an exit pupil number of 3.2 will have a relative brightness of 10.24 (3.2 multiplied by 3.2). A pair of binoculars with an exit pupil number of 5 will have a relative brightness of 25 (5×5).

It is also worth noting that when comparing the relative brightness of two pairs of binoculars, their brightness may actually differ if they have the same number depending on additional considerations such as prism type, lens coatings, etc.

4. Additional Considerations

While ancillary to the main specs, there are several other features to take into consideration when buying a pair of binoculars.

Eye Relief

Eye relief is the distance between your eyes and the viewing lenses (the lenses you peer through). The higher the number, the longer the eye relief, meaning you can hold the binoculars further from your face. This is especially important for those who wear glasses; these people should select a pair of binoculars with an eye relief of 11mm or more.

Field of View

The field of view of a pair of binoculars is the width of an area you can see 1,000 yards away. The higher the number, the wider the area. A wide field of view is important for bird watching and sports. The lower the magnification power (the first number in the primary specs), the wider the field of view is.

Focus

Just as one would focus a camera, binoculars feature a wheel that allows you to adjust the focus of what you're viewing. Typically, there is a focus wheel on each barrel of the binoculars which allows you to adjust each eye individually.

Prism Type

The prism inside a pair of binoculars is what allows the image to be oriented right-side up when viewing. There are two different types of prisms used: Porro and Roof. Porro prisms are less expensive and provide a good image but tend to be bulkier, adding size and weight. Roof prisms are smaller, lighter, and more expensive. Roof prisms are the de facto choice for backpackers.

Lens Coatings
Coatings are applied to lenses to help them be more efficient, allowing them to reflect less light and pull more light in, allowing images to appear brighter and crisper. Lenses that are multicoated do the best job at this.

Waterproof vs. Weather Resistant
Weather resistant binoculars are a good choice if you expect you may use your pair in light rain. Binoculars that are waterproof are suggested for use in heavy rain or on a boat, allowing them to be fully submerged without affecting their performance. Waterproof seals will also prevent dust and debris from entering and damaging your pair of binoculars.

Fog-proof
When transitioning between warm and cold temperatures, such as a warm car to the cold outdoors, lenses may fog up which can cause internal moisture to damage the binoculars. To combat this, manufacturers will add inert gas to the area inside the barrel between the lenses. Without any moisture content in these gases, the interior lenses

won't fog or become damaged.

Techie Language Explained

Barrel: A pair of binoculars has two barrels. Each barrel is a tube that holds both the objective lens and the lens that you peer through.

Focus Wheel: A small wheel that allows you to adjust the focus of the lenses to bring your intended object into view.

Turn-and-slide Eyecups / Adjustable Eyecups: These are another method of focusing your intended object, but allow each eye barrel to be adjusted individually.

Dielectric Coating: A versatile and high-quality lens coating that is used in a variety of devices such as binoculars, photography lenses, telescopes, and microscopes.

Product Recommendations

Wildlife enthusiasts looking to get a good glimpse of their favorite bird or scout for a brown bear will be well equipped with the *Celestron LandScout 12 – 36 x 60mm Spotting Scope*. It includes a rotating tripod mount that lets you swivel from one spot to the other without having to readjust your focus.

Car campers in need of a reliable and quality pair of binoculars should consider the *Nikon Prostaff 3S 10 x 42 Binoculars.* Waterproof and fog-resistant, this pair was built for the outdoors.

Backpackers wanting a magnified view without the added weight will love the *Vortex Solo 10 x 25 Monocular*. At just 5.6 oz. in overall weight, this monocular is fully multicoated and weatherproof for all your backcountry adventures.

Casual hikers that hit the trail just a few times a year who want a second set of eyes to capture stellar views up close will appreciate the *Celestron UpClose 8 x 21 Roof Binoculars*. These entry-level priced binoculars offer 11mm of eye relief, making them ideal for people with glasses too.

Winter backpackers braving harsh conditions need a rugged and waterproof pair of binoculars like the *Nikon Monarch*. Their ultrawide field of view and low light performance makes them an ideal companion.

To get the most up-to-date information, please visit our web article Best Compact Binoculars where you'll find the latest recommendations on binoculars. This list is updated every year.

19. CHARGERS

This one is a toss-up on whether a charger is an absolute necessity. It largely depends on the type of outing you'll be doing. More traditional backpackers and those getting away for a weekend in nature typically choose to forego what they consider a "luxury" in order to unplug. However, those that choose to leave the charger behind and unplug from technology are typically familiar with their intended trail and campsite.

On the other hand, backpackers, thru-hikers, and those tackling a new trail that they've never been on should consider the benefits of bringing a charger. Having a backup method to charge a phone and/or a GPS unit in an emergency situation or if you've gotten lost can be a huge help in making it out safely.

Things To Consider When Choosing A Charger

When considering how you'd like to charge your electronics, keep in mind there are two major components: the power source and the power storage.

1. Power Sources

There are a variety of power sources to choose from that you can use to charge up a rechargeable battery pack. The four most common are:

AC Power Outlet (Wall Outlet)
12-volt DC (Car Charger)
USB Outlet
Solar Panel

If you plan on using just a battery pack to recharge your devices, you'll have a limited amount of charges available before the battery pack itself needs recharging. Bringing just a battery pack can be a good backup option, but it will need to be charged ahead of time.

If you plan on doing an extended backpacking trip or a thru-hike, having a reliable and independent source to recharge your battery pack is imperative. One option is using a wood burning stove with a USB charger. The other more reliable option is using a solar panel.

2. Solar Panels

By far the most reliable off-grid power source, solar panels will allow you to recharge and store power in your battery pack for when your devices run out of power. Keep in mind, a solar panel is not a replacement for a rechargeable battery pack. This is because:

Not all solar panels can regulate the flow of electricity, which could potentially cause damage to your device (phone or GPS).

Sun isn't guaranteed – it's better to recharge a battery pack when the sun is available and store/save that power for later.

Types of Solar Chargers
Generally speaking, there are 3 types of solar chargers to choose from:

Solar Panel only
Solar Panel with an integrated storage system
Solar Panel with a separate battery pack

The last option (solar panel w/ separate battery

pack) will give you the greatest flexibility in terms of being able to leave the solar panel behind for short excursions or bring it along for longer treks. It also has the added benefit of being able to be recharged via USB, DC, or AC power if you come across a hostel or a town where recharging on the grid is possible.

Solar Panel Considerations

Size

The larger the panels, the faster and more efficiently you will be able to recharge your battery pack. There is a trade-off when determining your panel size as large panels are bulkier and heavier – so not great for backpacking.

Smaller panels are lighter and more compact, but won't charge as quickly and will struggle to charge in cloudy conditions. Depending on their size and where you are hiking, smaller panels could be attached to the top of your backpack, allowing you to recharge on the go.

Output Capacity

Measured in Watts, solar panels with a higher wattage will pull more power in a shorter amount of time but also cost more.

Solid or Flexible

Solid panels tend to be less expensive overall but flexible panels can be rolled up or folded for compact storage.

3. Rechargeable Battery Pack

When purchasing an independent battery pack, there are several key specs to keep in mind. Read below to find out what you should consider before buying.

Storage Capacity
The storage capacity that a battery pack is rated for will be measured in mAh (milliAmp hours). When buying a battery pack, compare its capacity to that of the device you're charging to understand how many charges you will be able to achieve.

For example, a 2200 mAh battery pack will be able to recharge a device with an 1100 mAh battery almost twice. The reason you probably won't get two full charges is because transferring electricity between devices isn't 100% efficient and some energy is lost in the process.

Power Output
Double check the power output when buying a battery pack to ensure that it will sufficiently charge your device. Measured in volts, the power output must be at least equal to your device's battery. If the power output is lower than your device's battery, then you may end up discharging your device instead of charging it.

Techie Language Explained

MPPT Technology: MPPT (Maximum Power Point Tracking) is a type of charge controller that is currently the most efficient in existence. A charge controller is the "brain" for a solar panel that helps it extract as much sunlight as possible. MPPT is able to do this even in low light conditions and when the winter sun is low and not as powerful.

IPX: A measure of water-resistance / waterproofing; the higher the number, the better it resists water.

IPX 1 – 4: Water resistant to small drops of water and light splashes

IPX 5 – 6: Water resistant to large and powerful blasts and sprays of water

IPX 7: Fully waterproof up to 3 feet (1 meter)

IPX 8: Fully waterproof in water over 3 feet (1 meter)

Product Recommendations

Weekend backpackers needing a reserve battery

pack that is both light and compact should consider the *BioLite Charge 40 USB Power Bank*. At just 11.6 oz., this battery pack can fully charge a cell phone four times, has two USB outputs to charge two devices at once, and is water resistant.

Budget-conscious backpackers needing a little extra juice at an entry-level price point will get the best bang for their buck with the *Skullcandy Stash Portable Battery Pack*. The 6,000 mAh battery provides up to 24 hours of extra charge and includes both USB-C and micro-USB connection types.

Weekend warriors backpacking for just a few days at a time who are in need of some solar support will love the *Goal Zero Venture 30 Power Bank + Nomad 7 Plus Solar Panel Kit*. At just 21.5 oz., this lightweight solar panel and battery combo will ensure you're always charged.

Thru-hikers looking for a lightweight solar panel may find the *Powertraveller Extreme Solar Charger* to be exactly what they need. Skipping the battery altogether, this direct panel-to-phone charger only weighs 10.2 oz. and can be attached to the top of your pack for on-the-go charging.

Car campers not worried about size or weight will appreciate the behemoth power bank that is the *Goal Zero Yeti 150*. This burly battery/mini generator is able to fully recharge a smartphone 15 times, a tablet six times, and a laptop twice.

To get the most up-to-date information, please visit our web article Best Hiking Solar Chargers where you'll find the latest solar charger recommendations. This list is updated every year.

20. KNIVES AND MULTI-TOOLS

Knives and multi-tools are pretty essential to the outdoor experience, providing an invaluable asset on the trail. They have a wide variety of applications, allowing you to prepare a meal, cut paracord, whittle a stick, make field repairs, and even assist in administering first aid in potentially life-threatening scenarios.

Knife Or Multi-Tool (Or Both?)

The question between the two is really one of specificity vs. generalist application. Multi-tools are very specific and have an intended tool for each type of task that it will excel at performing. However, some people find multi-tools to be too specific and thus many of the options within a multi-tool to be impractical.

On the other hand, knives are a general tool that can be used in so many ways: slicing, piercing, picking, carving, prying, digging, and screwing, just to name a few. The flip side is that a knife won't perform these applications as well as a multi-tool but it may offer better overall usability.

However, you don't necessarily have to choose between the two. Many people carry both a knife and a multi-tool on the trail to cover the widest range of possibilities.

Things To Consider When Choosing A Knife

Generally speaking, there are two basic types of knives: fixed-blade and pocket knives. The best knife for you will depend on what you intend to use it for the most.

1. Pocket Knives
Best For: Backpacking, Hiking, Small Tasks

Pocket knives offer a compact and lightweight option for carrying a blade. Able to fold into themselves, pocket knives are best suited to smaller tasks such as cutting paracord, making small repairs, and some first aid situations.

Features
The features listed here are options that may be available and are not necessarily mutually exclusive. That said, they are highly desirable when choosing a pocket knife.

Locking Blade: This is a must when choosing a blade that folds down as it increases safety by locking the blade in place once unfolded. This can give the feel of having a fixed-blade knife, although it isn't nearly as strong considering joints introduce weakness.

One-Handed Opening: Some pocket-knives include a small notch that makes it easy to unfold the blade with a single hand. This feature can be advantageous in spur of the moment situations or when you don't have a free hand available.

Assisted Opening: Similar to one-handed opening pocket-knives, an assisted opening knife has a mechanism that switches on and fully unfolds the blade as you begin to open it. They also include a safety feature to prevent accidental opening when stored closed/folded.

2. Fixed-Blade Knives
Best For: Cooking, Fishing, Hunting, Self-Defense

Offering more stability and ergonomic grip than a pocket-knife, fixed-blade knives are your go to for cooking, gutting/skinning animals, self-defense, major field repairs, and life-saving first aid.

Features
The following features for a fixed-blade knife are non-negotiable. Look for a knife that checks off each and every one of these features as it will maximize what you are able to accomplish. Since fixed-blade knives are heavier and not as compact as pocket-knives, having all of the following features will make the trade off in weight/size worth it.

Full Tang: A knife with a full tang means that it is made from a single, continuous piece of metal from the tip all the way through the handle to the opposite end. This provides increased durability, greater leverage, and versatility. Should the handle ever fall off your blade, it can be wrapped in paracord and still used safely. The same cannot be said for partial-tang constructions.

Sharp Pointed Tip: When going the fixed-blade route, having a sharp, pointed tip is essential for self-defense and hunting. A blunted or rounded tip won't be able to pierce fur nor can it be thrust forwards. Having a pointed tip is also useful for a variety of smaller tasks, such as making detailed cuts, grooves, and notches into a piece of wood. It's also more useful for repairing gear and prying things apart or picking at something that requires a sharp point to penetrate.

Single-Edged Blade with Flat-Ground Spine: While seemingly better, it is best to avoid double-edged blades. Having a single-edged blade with a flat spine (or topside) will increase the versatility of your fixed-blade knife. Benefits include being able to strike a fire-starting ferro-rod to start a fire; baton through pieces of wood (i.e. hammering the spine of the knife); and the ability to place your thumb on the spine to increase leverage when performing precise cuts. It's important that the spine is also flat-ground (at a 90° angle) as opposed to rounded or beveled when using on a fire-starting ferro-rod.

Flat Pommel: Also known as the butt of the knife, having a flat pommel will assist in hammering and pounding. Stay away from rounded or hooked pommels as they will not be able to effectively hammer something.

3. Blade Shape

When figuring out the right knife for you, blade shape plays an important and specific role. Not all blade shapes are created equally and each have their strong suits. Consider the following shapes:

Drop-Point
Best for all-around use and hunting, drop-point blades feature a spine that curves slightly down towards the tip. The result is a large blade area ideal for slicing and an easily-controlled blade tip.

Clip-Point
Characterized by a front tip that appears clipped off, a clip-point blade has a narrower and more precise tip designed to assist with detailed tasks. However, this increase in exaction results in trading off some of its strength when compared to drop-point blades.

Spear-Point
Balanced and symmetrical with the tip in the middle of the blade, a spear point is good for thrusting. As the name suggests, it is useful when attached to a stick to make a spear. It can come either single or double-edged, but single-edged is highly recommended.

Sheepsfoot / Santoku
Characterized by a downward sloping spine that meets the blade edge at a low and off-center tip,

this style of blade is designed to prevent accidental piercing due to its blunted/rounded tip. These blades excel at cutting, slicing, and chopping and are best used for cooking.

Tanto
Inspired by Japanese Samurai swords, the tanto shape has an exceptionally strong tip for prying and piercing tough objects, but lacks in its ability to slice.

Trailing-Point
In these blades, the spine curves upwards to a point that is higher than the handle. This provides a wide and oversized blade area that makes it excellent for slicing, skinning, and filleting.

4. Blade Materials

The materials that make up a blade are an important aspect to the overall quality and longevity of a knife. Hard steel, while difficult to sharpen, holds its edge really well and is less likely to rust. Soft steel, on the other hand, is much easier to sharpen and is less likely to corrode, but doesn't hold its edge nearly as well as hard steel, thus requiring more maintenance to stay sharp.

There are three categories by which a blade's material quality is measured:

Toughness: the ability to bend without breaking
Hardness: the ability to resist bending and how

well the blade will hold its edge
Corrosion Resistance: the ability to resist rust and corrosion

All three of these attributes have their pros and cons. When choosing a blade, it's important to know what you want out of the blade as these categories exist on a sliding scale. The more you get out of one attribute, the less you will get of another. For example, the more a blade is able to resist rust and corrosion, the less hardness or toughness you will get from it.

It's important to know that there is no perfect blade and that finding the right balance between these attributes can serve different purposes equally well.

Stainless Steel vs. High-Carbon

Generally speaking, there are two categories of steel: stainless and high-carbon. By far the most popular material for a knife, stainless steel is both rust and corrosion resistant, but can lack when it comes to holding an edge. Some people prefer the lesser common high-carbon steel, which offers superior hardness and toughness, but is more susceptible to corroding than stainless steel.

More specifically, there are several types of steel that can be used in a knife's construction. We have listed the most common ones below:

420HC
Toughness: Moderate

Hardness: Low
Corrosion Resistance: Moderate

Easy to sharpen and relatively rust resistant, 420HC stainless steel has trouble holding its edge compared to other types of steel. However, it has a fair amount of toughness and is not likely to break unless under extreme pressure.

154CM
Toughness: Moderate
Hardness: Moderate
Corrosion Resistance: Moderate

Widely considered to be a high-quality steel, 154CM offers the best balance of all three attributes. If you can find its cousin, CPM154, then you have found a gem that is considered absolutely superior to the rest.

S30V
Toughness: Moderate
Hardness: Low
Corrosion Resistance: Moderate

Considered a slight step down from 154CM, this steel also offers a balance between all three categories. Although less expensive, its edge is more likely to chip than 154CM.

1.4116
Toughness: High

Hardness: Low
Corrosion Resistance: High
This is the steel used in Swiss Army knives and is incredibly resistant to corrosion and rust. It's also extremely tough but lacks the ability to hold an edge for very long. However, it can be sharpened in minutes and this trade-off is considered by many to be well worth it for a small utility knife.

5. Handle Materials

There are 4 common materials used in your knife's handle and each have their trade-offs.

Wood: Sporting a decent grip and high aesthetic value, but prone to water damage

Plastic: Can be slippery, but affordable and water resistant

Rubber: Also sports a decent grip and is water resistant, but less durable

Stainless Steel: Durable and water resistant, but can be slippery and feel cold

Things To Consider When Choosing A Multi-Tool

The benefits of a multi-tool are numerous, giving you access to tackle a variety of tasks with precision. Keep in mind that not all multi-tools are exactly the same. Some have more specific tools for cycling or use in the kitchen, while more generic sets will have a wide-ranging variety of tool options. Consider these options when making a purchase to find what will best suit your intended activity.

1. Implements

Common Implements:

 Multiple Blades
 Flathead/Phillips Head Screwdriver
 Scissors
 Wire Cutter
 Saw
 File
 Bottle Opener
 Can Opener

Specific Implements:

 Corkscrew
 Tweezers
 Toothpick
 Wire Stripper
 Ruler
 Awl

2. Size

Multi-tools vary in size as well as what specific implements are offered. They are generally offered in 3 different sizes:

Keychain-Sized
A great option for ultralight enthusiasts, these small tools deliver some specific implements with a low weight cost. Keep in mind their small size does limit their strength and versatility, but many prefer a keychain size over nothing at all.

Pocket-Sized
A good middle ground that will appeal to most people, a pocket-sized multi-tool is a great option for backpackers looking for a wide array of implements at a reasonable weight.

Heavy Duty
Best suited for car campers, these mini toolboxes offer the most options with a hefty size for strength and ergonomic grip.

Techie Language Explained

Spine: The "top" side of a knife, opposite the blade edge on a single-edged knife. Double-edged knives have another blade edge where the spine would be.

Barrel Spacers: These hold the two sides of a handle together on a pocket-knife.

Carbon Fiber: A woven material known for its stiffness and durability. It is 3 times stiffer and 10 times stronger than steel.

Product Recommendations

Lightweight enthusiasts and thru-hikers searching to find the intersection of lightweight and utility are best suited with the *Benchmade 940-1 Osborne Carbon Fiber Locking Knife*. At just 2.4 oz., this knife is exceptionally light and boasts S90V steel, a big step up from S30V that holds its edge for a very, very long time.

Gadget junkies wanting specific tools in a lightweight design should consider the *Leatherman Skeletool Topo Multi-Tool*. At just 5 oz. and 4 in. long, this multi-tool sports all the primary implements with none of the fluff.

Car campers needing a hefty tool with just about every implement possible will appreciate the *Leatherman Surge Multi-Tool*. Boasting 15 implements, this hefty multi-tool is your second toolbox.

Backpackers looking for a no-frills fixed-blade knife will absolutely love the *Morakniv Garberg Multi-Mount Knife*. It hits all of the checkboxes listed above and sports 14C28N Sandvik stainless steel, which uses Nitrogen, instead of Carbon, to increase the hardness without the drawback of reduced corrosion-resistance.

Hunters and fishers looking for a solid blade that will skin, gut, slice, and dice should consider the *Benchmade 15400 Pardue Hunter Fine Edge Knife*. It features a full-tang design mated to a drop-point blade that will take care of your field dressing.

To get the most up-to-date information, please visit our web article Best Survival Multi-Tools where you'll find the latest multi-tool recommendations. This list is updated every year.

21. CAMERAS

Cameras for backpacking are as optional as they are for family vacations: they aren't vital but being able to capture memories and share them later is a pretty good reason to bring one. There are a variety of types of cameras and choosing the right one depends on what you want to get out of it. Having the right camera can give you the ability to properly document your adventure, make memories with friends and family, and share the wild scenery that you've experienced.

Things To Consider When Choosing A Camera

1. Types of Cameras

Point-and-Shoot
Pros: Easy to Use, Compact, Lightweight, Budget Friendly
Cons: Lower Quality, Smaller Sensors

A great option for the majority of backpackers, point-and-shoot cameras are easy to use, compact, and lightweight. Their budget friendly price point makes them less powerful than other options resulting in lesser quality images. However, if you're looking for an entry-level camera then this is a great choice.

Mirrorless
Pros: Great Quality, Affordable, Compact
Cons: Short Battery Life, Lack of Lenses, Subpar Autofocus

Mirrorless cameras offer arguably the best bang for your buck for amateur photos. Backpackers and campers wanting the quality of a DSLR camera in a lighter and more compact package should seriously consider this option.

DSLR

Pros: Superior Quality, Long Battery Life, Versatile, Shoots Video, Tons of Lenses
Cons: Large, Heavy, Very Expensive

The highest quality cameras around, DSLR (Digital Single-Lens Reflex) are what the pros use. If you're looking to break into photography as a career, then this is the type of camera you'll need.

Action Cameras
Pros: High Quality, Compact, Lightweight, Easy to Use, Waterproof, Shoots Video
Cons: Short Battery Life, Less Control Over Settings

A compact action camera may be just the right choice for your backpacking adventure. These rugged cameras can take both pictures and video and are waterproof. Just toss the cam in your bag, snag it before your day hike to a waterfall, and catch epic shots as you plunge into the water.

2. Additional Considerations

Depending on your intended use and the quality of images you'd like to capture, there are several other specs to consider before choosing a camera.

Size and Weight
The size and weight of your camera depends largely on your intended activity and what type of photographs you want to take. There is no hard rule on what size or how heavy your camera gear

should or shouldn't be, but there are some general recommendations.

Car campers and day hikers don't need to worry very much about size or weight. But if you're a backpacker, you will typically want to keep weight down in your pack.

If you're a backpacker looking to take casual photos, consider a point-and-shoot or an action camera. However, if your reason for backpacking is to get the best photos possible, then you will need a mirrorless or DSLR camera.

Mirrorless is probably the best intersection of quality and weight for backpackers if you're an amateur photographer. If professional photography is your ultimate goal, then a DSLR is your best bet. You'll just need to figure out how to shave weight in other places.

Megapixels and File Formats

Generally speaking, the more megapixels a camera has, the better-quality photos it will take. A higher megapixel count translates into a higher resolution and a bigger sized image file, meaning highly detailed and more vivid photos.

File formats are an important aspect of what camera you choose. In order to properly edit your photos with an editing software such as Adobe Premiere Pro or Lightroom, you will need a camera that can shoot RAW. This will give you greater control when editing in order to make truly professional grade photos. Of course, you don't have to shoot in RAW, but all cameras that shoot RAW are also able to shoot most other file formats as well.

Techie Language Explained

RAW: As opposed to JPEG (or JPG) format, which compresses and automatically optimizes your photo to make it easy to share widely across web platforms, shooting in RAW means that the photo you take is not adjusted, compressed, or optimized in any way by the camera itself, allowing you to edit it fully once you download the image to your computer. RAW files cannot be shared as easily as JPEG, but they are usually much higher quality.

Focal Length: The distance between the lens and the image formed on the film, measured in millimeters. Although film is rarely used anymore, lenses are still measured this way. The higher the number, the more "zoomed" in the picture will be.

File Format: How your camera will record the images taken. JPEG is a very common file type for images, but RAW is the preferred format for those who wish to edit the photo.

Automatic Mode: Automatic mode on a camera gives you less control over the photo being taken and allows the software in the camera to adjust the exposure settings. While this can help a novice take a decent photo, it is extremely limited in capabilities.

Manual Mode: Manual mode on a camera allows you to manipulate the exposure settings (Aperture, Shutter Speed, and ISO), giving you greater control over the photo.

Shutter Release: The button that actually takes the photo.
Viewfinder: The hole you look through to take the photo. Almost all cameras have one in addition to the digital screen that is also usually found on the camera body.

Product Recommendations

Ultralight backpackers and thru-hikers who know that every ounce is precious but still want to be able to snag some cool photos and videos along the way will appreciate the *GoPro HERO7 Black*. It's waterproof, grab-n-go, mount-it-anywhere versatility makes it the ideal lightweight companion.

Car campers looking for a simple, yet rugged, point-and-shoot camera ought to consider the *Olympus TG-5 Waterproof* camera. Its straightforward and easy to use design makes it great for the family and its waterproof body protects it for more adventurous hikes.

Wildlife photographers looking to create stunning visuals will get the most out of a *Canon EOS 5D Mark IV*. It's 30-megapixel sensor maximizes the colors being captured and make editing much more fun.

Casual outdoor photographers looking to get the best bang for their buck under $500 will find the *Canon PowerShot G9X Mark II* to be a great option. It's 20 megapixels packed into a small point-and-shoot body make it ideal for travel, casual camping trips, and family beach days.

Aspiring cinematographers looking for a camera that captures stunning 4K video and takes amazing photos will want to reach for the *Sony Alpha A7S II*. This mirrorless camera sports every bell and whistle in a smaller body, making it perfect for the adventurous types.

To get the most up-to-date information, please visit our web articles Best Cameras for Landscape Photography, Best Cameras for Wildlife Photography and Best Cameras for Travel Photography where you'll find the latest camera recommendations. These lists are updated every year.

SECTION VII: SAFETY

22. FIRST AID KITS

A well-stocked first aid kit is one of the most important resources to bring with you on the trail. Whether you're out for a short day-hike or venturing into the wilderness for days/weeks on end, a first aid kit is a simple and effective first line of defense.

Things To Consider When Buying Or Building A First Aid Kit

First aid kits can be either bought or built. Buying one from a trusted outdoor retailer provides convenience and peace of mind that you will have all the right resources. Store bought first aid kits also come with a rating for the number of people it will serve and how many days it will last. This added benefit takes a lot of the guesswork out of building your own kit.

Check Before You Go

Whether you've purchased a complete kit or pieced together your own first aid kit, it's a good idea to develop the habit of checking the contents of your kit before leaving on your trip. There are 3 benefits to this:

> You will be familiar with what's in your kit
> You'll have the opportunity to restock expired or soon-to-be-expired items
> You can create a trip specific kit

Being familiar with the contents of your kit, and how to use each item, is important when it comes time to use them. By knowing each item, you can make the call on how to customize your kit how you see fit.

Finding that medicine or other items are expired while on the trail is the last place you want to learn that information. Checking your kit before you leave will afford you the opportunity to restock with fresh supplies.

Not all first aid kits need to be identical. Think about the activities you'll be doing in order to create a trip specific kit. For example, if your hike leads you to a bouldering spot, a simple hiking first aid kit likely won't have everything you need. Assess the most common minor and major injuries that can occur from bouldering/climbing and add the appropriate supplies to your kit.

Another example is if your trip includes river crossings or paddling, where water would be prone to damaging your supplies or rendering regular adhesive bandages useless. Consider adding waterproof adhesive bandages to your kit as well as securing your kit in a dry bag.

Supplies

Basic Care
Antiseptic Wipes (BZK-based wipes)
Antibacterial Ointment
Antihistamine
Treats allergic reactions
Assortment of Bandages
Adhesive Bandages
Butterfly Strips
Assortment of Pain Relief Medication
Aspirin or Ibuprofen (non-steroidal anti-inflammatory drug; NSAID)
Tylenol (pain reliever/fever reducer)
Benzoin Compound Tincture

Blister Treatment
Gauze Pads
Non-Stick Sterile Pads
Medical Adhesive Tape
Bug Sting/Anti-Itch Treatment
Afterbite
Poison Ivy/Oak Scrub
Fine Point Tweezers
Safety Pins
Menstruation
First Aid Manual

Advanced Care
Cohesive Wrap
Conforming Stretch Bandage
Elastic Bandage
Hemostatic Agent (such as QuickClot, Celox, and HemCon)
Used to clot blood and stop bleeding in major wounds
Hydrogel Pads (Used for abrasions, severe scrapes, minor burns, or where a wound/injury should be kept moist)
Liquid Bandage
Rolled Gauze
Splints
Finger Splint
SAM Splint
Triangular Cravat Bandage

Medications & Treatments
Aloe Vera Burn Relief (Gel or Spray)

Anti-Diarrheal Medication
Antacid Tablets
Glucose/Sugar Packets (Used to treat hypoglycemia)
EpiPen
Lubricating Eye Drops
Oral Rehydration Salts
Personal Prescription Medications

Tools & Supplies
Biodegradable Soap
Hand Sanitizer
Cotton-Tipped Swabs
CPR Mask
Irrigation Syringe for cleaning debris and dirt out of wounds
Medical Shears (Blunt Tipped)
Notepad w/ Waterproof Pencil (To keep patient notes, list of symptoms, time log of patient's progress or worsening symptoms throughout the day)
Oral Thermometer
Razor Blade
Surgical Gloves (nitrile, not latex)
Space Blanket/Emergency Shelter

Unusual/Creative First Aid Supplies
Superglue. It can be used to keep large wounds closed when stitches are required.

Small Roll of Duct Tape. Infinite versatility including makeshift sling, extra medical tape, etc.

Tampon. In an emergency situation can be used to plug a large puncture or laceration.

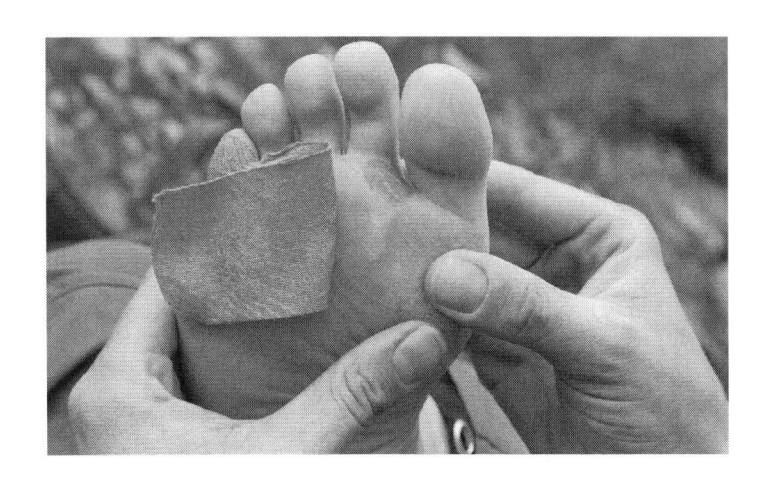

23. FOOT CARE

Taking proper care of your feet is paramount when it comes to spending time on the trail. Your feet are your most precious resource considering that they're your sole mode of transportation. The best defense for avoiding blisters, frostbite, and other foot pain is to properly care for your feet ahead of time, outlined below. An ounce of prevention is worth a pound of cure.

If you do happen to end up with a blister, we've also outlined how to treat those as well.

Preventative Care

1. Cleanliness.
Clean your feet often!

Many backpackers take a 15-minute break 2 – 4 times over the course of a full day of hiking to hydrate and refuel, but many neglect to free their feet. When taking one of these strategic stops (as well as during lunch time), the first and best thing you can do is to remove your boots and socks. Not only does this give your sweaty feet and socks a chance to air out, but you can shake out dirt and pebbles that tend to be the main culprit for blisters.

Before hitting the sack each night, washing your feet with biodegradable soap will help prevent dirt and grime from building up day after day. Once dry, finish them off with a drop of hand sanitizer to prevent any possibility of bacterial growth. Maintaining clean and dry feet will carry you further with less chances for problems further down the trail.

2. Moisturize.
Soft feet are happy feet!

Moisturizing your feet each night will go a long way towards the overall health of your feet. Not only does it feel nice, but it can also help your feet feel warmer in cold environments. After you've thoroughly washed and sanitized your feet, and after your dirty socks have dried out, apply either lotion or salve to your feet before pulling your socks back on.

Although this is an unusual regimen for foot care, it goes a long way in making your feet feel warmer at night and better overall. Moisturizing will also prevent your feet from cracking and bleeding in dry and winter climates.

3. Stretch & Exercise
Self-care applies to feet too!

Just as you would stretch, exercise, and occasionally massage your body to prepare, maintain, and take care of it for any sports, your feet are no different when it comes to hiking. What works for major muscle groups also works for your feet.

Doing toe stands, toe curls, and walking on soft sand will serve to strengthen your feet and condition them for hiking. Rolling a tennis ball beneath the soles of your feet will help work out any knots or pain and stretching your Achilles tendons will help alleviate any tightness or pain in your heels.

Massaging your feet regularly is perhaps the easiest way to provide relief and relax your feet. Make it a habit to massage your feet as often as possible on the trail (before bed, in the morning at breakfast, and on the trail during a break) and it will pay dividends in your overall foot health.

4. Comfort

You'll only perform as well as you feel, and the same logic applies when properly caring for your feet. Make sure you have comfortable hiking boots/shoes that are broken in well before a big trip. Starting a long hike with a brand-new pair of boots is never a good idea. Instead, take smaller day hikes and wear them around town for an hour or two at a time to gently break them in. This will help avoid blisters in the future.

The types of socks you wear may just be even more important than the style of hiking boot or shoe you wear. Wool socks are the most durable, the most efficient at wicking sweat, and the best at keeping your feet warm when compared to synthetic blended socks. Never, under any circumstances, should you wear cotton socks while hiking.

Treatment

A blister forms when there is too much heat, friction, pressure, moisture, or combination thereof applied to your skin. The outermost layer of your skin separates from the next layer down and fluid fills the space between in an attempt to heal the damaged skin.

1. Listen to Your Feet

If you feel an uncomfortable spot on your feet when hiking, you should immediately stop and remove your socks and shoes. Let your feet dry out and inspect them for "hot spots" (red irritated areas). Catching hot spots early affords you the opportunity to treat them before they become painful blisters. The treatment for hot spots is very similar to treating full blown blisters (as outlined below): you can choose to apply tape, blister bandage pads, or moleskin.

2. How to Treat a Blister

Moleskin
Cut the moleskin into the shape of a doughnut, with a hole large enough to fit the entire blister. The foam moleskin will protect the area around the blister while also reducing the pressure against the actual blister itself.

Blister Pads
Blister pads usually have a cooling gel agent in the pad. Applying a pad to the blistered area will provide a protective layer while helping the area cool down.

Draining (if necessary)
As a general rule, it's best to leave a blister alone

since the fluid in the blister is attempting to heal the damaged area of skin. Draining the blister slows down this process and increases the potential for infection (since you will most likely be putting your foot back into a warm/moist boot – the perfect conditions for bacterial growth).

However, if a blister becomes too painful to continue hiking, follow these steps. If the blister pops on its own, skip to step 5.

1 - Wash the blistered area with biodegradable soap and disinfect with hand sanitizer

2 - Sterilize a needle by wiping it down with an alcohol swab, holding it over an open flame such as a lighter for 10 – 15 seconds, or boiling it in water for 10 minutes.

3 - Slide the needle into the bottom of the blister at an angle parallel with your skin (so as not to accidentally prick yourself).

4 - Gently drain the fluid.

5 - Add a moleskin doughnut over the area with a hole large enough to fit the entire blister

6 - Apply antibiotic ointment to the exposed blister (the doughnut hole area) and cover with an adhesive bandage or a blister pad.

7 - Apply tape over the bandage or pad to provide extra support.

It's important to carry foot care materials with you on the trail such as moleskin, blister pads, adhesive bandages, and toe-nail clippers, but hopefully if you treat your feet well while hiking then you'll be able to prevent blisters from forming in the first place!

24. REPAIR KITS

Wear and tear of a hiker's gear is as certain as "death and taxes" are for every citizen. To that end, having a basic kit to make field repairs will ensure that minor setbacks stay minor and don't slow you down. Considered one of the most essential items for any and every hiker to have, a field repair kit is an inexpensive insurance policy to keep you on the go.

Things To Have In Your Repair Kit

The following list is a limited inventory of items to have in your repair kit. Feel free to get creative and add other supplies at your discretion.

50 ft. Paracord
Usually found in clever design such as a paracord bracelet, these utilitarian bracelets can be unwound to provide you with a lightweight yet highly durable rope for lashing, tying, cinching, and bundling gear.

Alcohol Wipes
Use these to clean any dirty area before applying an adhesive such as duct tape, superglue, seam sealer, or a repair patch. It will help the agent properly bond to the material you're repairing.

Duct Tape
Duct tape is the king of repair supplies and can be used in countless ways in a pinch. Wrap 3 – 5 feet of it around hiking poles or a water bottle to keep it handy without taking up unnecessary space in your pack.

Extra Buckle(s)
A broken buckle on a key area of your pack can comprise the entire system and make hiking

much more difficult. To avoid this problem, identify the types/sizes of buckles on your multi-day pack and plan to have at least one backup of each size.

Lighter
Similar to duct tape, a lighter is useful for a variety of scenarios, especially for searing the ends of freshly cut rope to avoid fraying.

Outdoor Sewing Kit
These small tackle boxes will expand your repair capabilities when glue or tape won't remedy the situation. Many include thread and needle, extra buttons, safety pins, and even a crash course on sewing.

Stove Service Kit
Check to see if your stove's manufacturer has a service kit. These typically include a variety of replacement parts such as O-rings, springs, plugs, injector lines, and more. Having a kit of this nature is a major boon if your stove breaks down.

Superglue
Similar to duct tape, superglue can repair a variety of problems in a pinch, especially if something plastic has snapped. Your creativity will determine just how many ways it can be applied on the trail.

Tenacious Tape Repair Patches
When tape or glue won't cut it, a repair patch can

save your sleeping bag, stuff sack, tent wall, rainfly, hammock, and more.

Tent Pole Splint

Since most tent pole systems are interconnected and rely on each other, a snapped pole can compromise the integrity of the entire tent. A small aluminum tent pole splint can easily mend this problem – just slide it over the broken spot and tape it up.

Waterproof Seam Sealer

While superglue can bond to many surfaces, there are some it just won't bond to. Cover all your bases by snagging a waterproof seam sealer that is specifically designed to adhere to leather, nylon, neoprene, PVC, rubber, and vinyl.

Zip Ties

Makeshift shoe-laces, broken buckle conjoiner, impromptu straps: the possibilities are endless as to what zip ties can be used for when backpacking.

25.
COMMUNICATION DEVICES

There isn't a straightforward answer when asking if one really needs a communication device while backpacking or camping. As with many things, it all depends. If you're car camping or backpacking a familiar trail that isn't too challenging, then leaving communication technology at home is fine.

However, if your outdoor pursuits take you deep into remote areas, if you will be traversing treacherous trail, or if bad weather has the potential to increase your risk, then bringing along a communication device may be in your best interest. Being able to send a distress call to emergency professionals or simply being able to make contact with other members of your expedition can provide a much-needed backup when things go south.

Things To Consider When Choosing A Communication Device

There are three types of communication devices you can bring along with you in the backcountry: Two-Way Radios, Personal Locator Beacons, and Satellite Messengers. Each one varies greatly as to intended use and the features provided.

It's important to keep in mind that cell phones should NOT be relied on as a primary means of communication, especially when backpacking in remote areas and attempting a thru-hike. Cell towers are still limited in national parks, rural areas, and remote wilderness and even when they are present, mountains and dense wilderness are enough to block signals or provide interference.

To have the best chances of surviving in an

emergency situation, consider either a Personal Locator Beacon (PLB) or a Satellite Messenger.

1. Two-Way Radios

Size and Weight
Two-way radios come in a variety of sizes and weight. For camping and backpacking it's best to find a lightweight and compact sized radio to reduce overall weight.

Radio Channels
Two-way radios used for outdoor recreation usually have up to 22 channels that can be utilized on one of two available bands: Family Radio Service (FRS) band or General Mobile Radio Service (GMRS) band. The latter requires a 10-year license to be obtained by the FCC (Federal Communications Commission).

Wattage and Range Coverage
Although many radios boast of having a range of up to 25 miles, this only occurs in ideal environments rather than real-world conditions. Realistically, the range will probably be about 1 – 2 miles.

When determining the best type of radio for your needs, you'll be deciding between FRS and GMRS band. More casual backpackers looking to keep in touch with friends on the trail should opt for the FRS band. At ½ Watt, the range will be roughly 5 – 6 miles (a pretty good range) and will also be lighter and less expensive.

For those needing maximal range, a GMRS band radio at 1 – 2 Watts will cover between 8 – 25 miles. These high-powered radios offer stronger signal even when interference would disrupt a weaker radio. However, these two-way radios are much pricier and run through battery much quicker than FRS band radios.

Features

There are a wide array of features that can make or break the particular two-way radio you need. Below we've compiled a list of the most common features and how they help overall usability.

Calling and Paging Features

Some models offer the ability to beep or make a sound before communication is received. This lets the person on the receiving end of the transmission know that information is incoming.

Keypad Lock

Keypad locks offer a convenient way to ensure your settings aren't changed as your move about.

Noise Filter

This built-in feature helps increase your range coverage and provides stronger signals.

Scanning

A quick way to find an empty channel for your party to use.

Radio/GPS Combo Units

Some two-way radios are built into a GPS unit, offering a combo that reduces your overall weight. One of the unique features of these devices is peer-to-peer positioning, which allows your friends to see your coordinates.

Texting GPS Units
These units allow you to connect a cell phone and text to others with the same set-up instead of the speak-and-listen setup of traditional two-way radios.

VOX
Although typically more suited for skiers and mountain bikers, a voice activated (VOX) feature lets you communicate hands free. This feature is also desirable for mountain climbers. Some radios also include a headphone jack that offers similar functionality.

Weather Radio
This is an essential feature for backcountry backpackers and thru-hikers; it gives you access to NOAA (National Oceanic & Atmospheric Administration) weather band stations to stay up to date on local weather conditions and forecasts.

2. Personal Locator Beacon (PLB)

A PLB is a simplified device that doesn't really let you communicate, rather it's like a high-tech flare gun that allows you to send an SOS during an emergency.

Features
PLB's are satellite connected and allow you to send an SOS to professional emergency personnel. Some of their key features are:

No subscription fees
Work in all U.S. remote areas
Work in most remote areas worldwide
Stronger signal than a satellite messenger
Single use battery with a life span of many years

How it Works
A PLB is like a dormant system that you keep on you in case of emergency. When an emergency scenario arises, you activate your PLB which in turn sends a powerful distress signal to a system of satellites.

Once your signal is received, the distress call is passed through a series of emergency response agencies where it is eventually filtered to the proper rescue team based upon your location and particular type of situation. Many PLBs also communicate your GPS-coordinates to the emergency response team to increase chances of rescue.

Registration
All PLBs must be registered with the NOAA's SARSAT (Search and Rescue Satellite Aided Tracking) database. This doesn't cost anything and is a huge benefit to you. Registration gives search and rescue teams access to vital information (name, ad-

dress, emergency contact, and pertinent medical information) that will help their efforts.

Your registration must be updated every 2 years and the database needs to be notified if you ever sell or transfer your PLB. This will then make way for the next person to register that PLB.

Battery Life
The batteries used in PLBs are very unique, as they lie dormant until the PLB is activated in an emergency situation. The lithium-battery can last for up to 5 years, making it low-hassle and eliminating the need to recharge it. Once the PLB is activated, government regulations specify that Class 2 batteries must be able to continually transmit a signal for 24 hours in temperatures down to -20°F. Since this represents an extreme scenario, it is likely that most Class 2 batteries will transmit your signal for at least 30 hours or more in temperate weather.

3. Satellite Messenger

Unlike a PLB, satellite messengers are more technologically advanced devices that do allow advanced communication such as texting and sending emails. They can also send an SOS during an emergency situation.

Features
Satellite messengers have a base of standard features, including:

Rechargeable batteries
Requires a subscription
Some models offer GPS navigation
The ability to send and receive texts/emails
Works in remote areas worldwide with coverage varying by company
Select units offer two-way texting with emergency personnel to coordinate extraction (can also be used to cancel an SOS)

Many satellite messengers also now include more advanced features such as:

Topo-map navigation
Real-time weather data/reports
Pair to your smartphone via Bluetooth
Sync and control device via a fitness watch
Waypoint tracking and progress reports sent to loved ones

How it Works
Satellite messengers rely on networks of satellites, both commercial and GPS, for communication and location, respectively. SOS calls are routed through a private company headquarters called GEOS based in Houston, Texas (International Emergency Response Coordination Center) who then coordinate efforts with the proper search and rescue agencies. They are also able to communicate updates with you in real-time.

Considering international expeditions, it all

depends on what country you're in and the resources available to the local search and rescue teams. Check with the manufacturer of your device to see what international coverage is provided. Also, be aware that some countries have banned GPS devices. Make sure you know the laws of the country you'll be visiting and plan accordingly.

Subscription
Satellite messengers require pricey subscription plans in order to work but considering that you're tapping into a premium network that pulls out all the stops, these plans offer the best bang for your buck.

If you're planning on being in remote areas for extended periods of time (30+ days), especially outside of the U.S., these subscriptions are your safest bet. Many of them offer a type of insurance that can cover search and rescue expenses up to $50,000 and MEDEVAC benefits up to $1 million. Some will even offer a risk assessment of your travel itinerary, pre-travel security advice, and security evacuations.

The plans and rates can vary quite a bit depending on your provider. Be sure to check what is offered and compare prices before buying.

Battery Life
Battery life can range between a few days to almost 3 weeks, but the upside is that batteries are rechargeable. This can be great if you have occa-

sional stops in civilization to recharge, but also means you will need to balance battery usage with trip duration on more remote expeditions. You don't want emails to drain your battery for a potential emergency!

Techie Language Explained

IPX: A measure of water-resistance / waterproofing; the higher the number, the better it resists water.

IPX 1 – 4: Water resistant to small drops of water and light splashes

IPX 5 – 6: Water resistant to large and powerful blasts and sprays of water

IPX 7: Fully waterproof up to 3 feet (1 meter)

IPX 8: Fully waterproof in water over 3 feet (1 meter)

Iridium Satellite Network: A network of privately-owned satellites in lower Earth orbit that provide cell and data coverage across the entire world no matter how remote your location is.

Topo-Maps: A topographic map shows the features of the earth, including but not limited to: roads, trails, bodies of water, buildings, boundaries, mountains, vegetation type, terrain, and slope. These are incredibly useful for planning a route as they can show you the limits, extremes, and possibilities for your path.

Product Recommendations

Thru-hikers needing a lightweight emergency backup plan may want to snag the *ACR Electronics ResQLink 400*. At just 5.3 oz., this ultra-tough weatherproof PLB will give you peace of mind should an emergency arise.

Large groups of backpackers looking to stay in touch with each other on the trail should consider the *Motorola Talkabout T800*. Delivering up to 2 Watts of power on GMSR band stations, this two-way radio will also allow you to share your location with your travel companions.

Extended trip (30+ days) backpackers and those wading into extremely remote environments should spring for the *Garmin inReach Satellite+ 2-Way satellite Communicator*. Its 100-hour battery gives you enough power to communicate with family, share location, download topo-maps from the cloud, and send distress calls to GEOS.

Car campers needing a simple way to keep track of friends and family should snag the *Motorola T100 Two-Way Radio*. Its simplified design makes it easy to use and offers access to all 22 channels.

Winter backpackers needing a PLB that will work in extreme conditions will benefit greatly from the *ACR Electronics AquaLink View PLB*. This tech-savvy flare gun uses GPS to hone-in on your location within 100 meters and also sports an LED strobe light to help rescuers find you more easily.

To get the most up-to-date information, please visit our web article Best 2-Way Radios where you'll find the latest radio recommendations. This list is updated every year.

SECTION VIII: HYGIENE

26. CAMP BATHROOMS

At some point on the trail will come a time when you need to relieve yourself. Obey your body and oblige it – DO NOT try to hold it in. This is both uncomfortable and dangerous. Below, we've outlined how to take care of business in the backwoods.

Urinating

Where to Go
Choose a site 200 feet (70 paces) away from all trails, campsites, and water sources

Never go directly in a body of water

When camping at high altitudes, peeing on a large rock is best. This will help deter goats from digging up fragile vegetation to get to the salt that urine leaves behind

If you're camping in a cold climate or wintery weather, consider bringing an empty plastic bottle to use as a "pee bottle" so you can avoid leaving your tent at night. Then you can empty the bottle in the morning.

FEMALE CONSIDERATIONS

Items You'll Need
Toilet Paper or Bandana (Pee Rag)
Plastic Ziplock-type Bags
Pee Funnel (optional)

Streamlining the Process
Find a soft spot on the earth to pee – this will help minimize backsplash when squatting

Wide Stance = Better Balance

Squat Uphill, Aim Downhill – on uneven terrain, this will keep you out of the way of the downhill stream

Consider using a pee funnel which allows you to pee while standing up – this will provide ease and convenience

Used toilet paper should be stored in a plastic baggy and disposed of at home

A bandana used as a pee rag is a low maintenance alternative to toilet paper – simply tie it to the exterior of your pack to allow it to dry and rinse when you're able to

Defecating

It's not uncommon for a pooping regimen to change while on the trail. You're stressing the body in ways that it's not used to and typically eating and drinking differently than you would at home. Not to mention that the body uses its available resources extremely efficiently and as such, you may produce less excrement.

If you haven't pooped in a couple of days on the trail, fret not. Being "regular" is considered as having a bowel movement anywhere in the range of once every three days to three times per day. Any more or less than this range is cause for concern.

It is also incredibly important that you become comfortable pooping in nature. Attempting to "hold it" until the trip is over is not only uncomfortable, but dangerous for your body.

Items You'll Need
Trowel (for digging/covering up your cat hole)
Several Plastic Ziplock-type Bags (larger is better)
Toilet Paper or Baby Wipes
Hand Sanitizer
Solid Waste Bag/Blue Bag (if human waste must be packed out)

Where to Go
Choose a site 200 feet (70 paces) away from all trails, campsites, and water sources

Your drop site should consist of soft soil and be in the sun if possible. Beneath a rock is a suitable alternative when the ground is densely packed or mostly clay

If none of the above are available, be prepared to pack out your waste

Doing the Deed
When digging a cat hole, it should be roughly 4" inches wide and 6" – 8" inches deep – some trowels come with a ruler to help you measure your hole.

For a rough estimate of size, make a fist with your hand and extend the pinky and thumb to make the "shaka" sign. The distance between your extended pinky and thumb is a rough estimate for how deep and wide the hole should be.

Check to make sure where you're camping allows the cat hole method. Some areas require all human waste to be packed out especially if the area is ecologically sensitive, highly trafficked, or high in elevation.

Cleanup
If using toilet paper:
Try to use as little toilet paper as possible – place toilet paper in the cat hole after wiping and bury with dirt. Tamp down the dirt with your boot and consider placing a rock on top.

If using baby wipes:
Baby wipes must be packed out – place them in a plastic baggy for safe disposal. Bury your payload with dirt and tamp down your boot; consider placing a rock on top.

Hygiene
You should always clean your hands after pooping, whether you use biodegradable soap or hand sanitizer. It will ensure you don't contaminate anything or get sick on the trail. If camping with friends, ask someone else to pour water and soap on your hands after going to avoid cross-contamination of your water source.

27. FEMININE HYGIENE

Just because your period is coming doesn't mean that should exclude you from being able to lead an epic backpacking trip. Being prepared with a few essential supplies, a little planning ahead, and knowledge of the Leave No Trace Principles will ensure that your trip runs smoothly.

Things To Consider Regarding Feminine Hygiene

Supplies

Each woman has her preference when it comes to choosing the right tool for the job. However, being on the trail may introduce difficulties that you're not used to dealing with. Consider the following supplies to determine which will work best for you.

Tampons/Pads
Since these are the most commonly used supplies, chances are you're familiar with using them. If that's what you feel most comfortable using, then it's probably best to keep the same routine.

One potential drawback, however, is the weight and space that these supplies take up in your pack. Also, be sure that you pack out all of your used tampons/pads in a plastic baggy/waste bag. Leave No Trace Principles don't allow them to be buried in a cat hole since animals are prone to digging them up.

Menstrual Cup
A menstrual cup offers a great opportunity to reduce waste and simplify what goes into your Go Kit, as well as reduce your overall pack weight.

However, it's advised that you practice using your cup at home for a couple of periods before attempting to use it in the wilderness. If using a cup, make sure you also have biodegradable soap and surgical gloves to make cleanup easier.

Go Kit

A Go Kit is simply a streamlined system that consists of your menstrual products, a waste bag, and cleaning supplies. All fit within your Go Kit to make it an easy Grab-and-Go Kit.

Clean Bag

Many women choose to use a small 4 Liter stuff sack to hold all of their supplies in one place.

You should include the following in your clean bag:

Several zip-lock bags to hold tampons/pads (if you're using these supplies)
Pack of sanitary wipes
Hand Sanitizer
Biodegradable Soap (for washing hands and soiled clothing)
Disposable Surgical Gloves (nitrile)

Waste Bag

The best waste bags are plastic baggies with zip-tops that will ensure nothing leaks. Consider adding coffee grounds or baking soda to help mitigate any potential odors. You may also line the bag with aluminum foil or duct tape to keep waste more hidden. Make sure that all used supplies, including pads, tampons, and any sanitary wipes and/or disposable gloves go into the bag when you're finished.

To get the most up-to-date information, please visit our web article Female Hygiene Guide for Hiking and Camping.

SECTION IX:
CHECKLISTS

28. SUMMER DAY-HIKE

Day hikes can range anywhere from 4 – 16 miles roundtrip and can take a half to a full day to accomplish. When hiking in the summer, there are several things you need to keep in mind, including outside temperature, timing, hydration, and nutrition.

When taking a day hike in the summer, keep an eye on the temperature throughout the day. The hottest part of the day is typically in the afternoon, so time your hike accordingly. Either plan to go early in the morning and be done before the afternoon, or if you have a long hike ahead of you, then make sure to plan for a lengthy break at midday. You may also choose to hike in the evening, perhaps to view the sunset from a vista, after the temperature has dropped enough to be comfortable. If hiking later in the day, make sure to carry a headlamp and an extra warm layer in your pack in case you find yourself hiking back in the dark.

Also, be sure to hydrate well the night before and the morning of your hike, as well as intermittently throughout your trek. Eat salty snacks on the trail to help you retain fluids and take breaks every 15 – 20 minutes to avoid heat stroke or heat exhaustion. Seek out shade as often as possible for your breaks and don't forget to slather on the sunscreen before you head out!

You can download this checklist in high-quality (print-ready) format at:

https://www.theadventurejunkies.com/gear-book-bonus

THE ADVENTURE JUNKIES

PACKING LIST:
SUMMER DAY HIKE

Essential: You need it to go hiking
Safety: Not essential, but it increases your safety
Comfort: Not essential, but can make the hike more enjoyable

BAGS & APPAREL

	ESSENTIAL	SAFETY	COMFORT
☐ Day Pack	√		
☐ Pack Rain Cover			√
☐ Moisture-Wicking T-Shirt	√		
☐ Long Sleeve Shirt with UPF		√	√
☐ Quick-Drying Pants / Shorts	√		
☐ Lightweight Fleece or Jacket			√
☐ Moisture-Wicking Underwear	√		
☐ Socks (Synthetic or Wool)	√		
☐ Hiking Boots / Sandals / Sneakers	√		
☐ Rain Jacket / Waterproof Layer		√	√
☐ Rain Pants			√
☐ Gaiters			√
☐ Bandana / Buff			√
☐ Sun Hat	√		

TOOLS & ACCESSORIES

	ESSENTIAL	SAFETY	COMFORT
☐ Trekking Poles		√	√
☐ Headlamp		√	
☐ Binoculars			√
☐ Chargers		√	
☐ Knife / Multi-Tool			√
☐ Camera			√
☐ Camera Hood / Rain Cover			√
☐ Extra Batteries		√	
☐ Fitness Tracker			√

FOOD & WATER

	ESSENTIAL	SAFETY	COMFORT
☐ Water Bottle / Hydration Reservoir	√		
☐ Water Treatment System		√	
☐ Lunch / Snacks			√
☐ Emergency Supply of Food		√	
☐ Camping Stove			√
☐ Stove Fuel			√
☐ Matches or Lighter			√
☐ Cookware			√
☐ Cutlery			√
☐ Waste Bag	√		

NAVIGATION & COMMUNICATION

	ESSENTIAL	SAFETY	COMFORT
☐ Map / Compass		√	
☐ GPS		√	
☐ Two-Way Radio		√	
☐ PLB / Satellite Radio		√	
☐ Hiking Guide		√	
☐ Watch		√	

SAFETY & REPAIR

	ESSENTIAL	SAFETY	COMFORT
☐ First Aid Kit		√	
☐ Lighter / Matches / Fire Starter		√	
☐ Bear Spray		√	
☐ Emergency Shelter		√	
☐ Whistle		√	
☐ Trail Route Itinerary Left With a Friend		√	

HEALTH & HYGEINE

	ESSENTIAL	SAFETY	COMFORT
☐ Sunscreen	√		
☐ Sunglasses	√		
☐ Chapstick / Lip Balm (w / SPF)			√
☐ Insect Repellant			√
☐ Hand Sanitizer		√	
☐ Baby Wipes			√
☐ Rubbing Alcohol / Antiseptic Wipes		√	
☐ Prescription Medication		√	
☐ Over the Counter Medication (i.e. Aspirin)			√
☐ Toilet Paper			√
☐ Urinary Products			√
☐ Menstruation Products			√
☐ Trowel			√
☐ Blister Treatment			√

PERSONAL ITEMS

	ESSENTIAL	SAFETY	COMFORT
☐ Field Journal w/ Pen / Pencil			√
☐ Personal Identification Card		√	
☐ Cell Phone		√	
☐ Cash / Credit Card	√		
☐ Hammock			√
☐ Picnic Blanket			√

29. WINTER DAY-HIKE

Considering the wide range of day hikes when it comes to duration (anywhere from 4 – 16 miles roundtrip), winter tends to slow your hiking pace especially if there's snow on the ground. You may need special gear to keep traction that you wouldn't normally require during summer hikes, such as crampons, trekking poles, snowshoes, or an ice axe.

When bundling up for colder temperatures, be

sure to have multiple layers that can easily be shed/added. In fact, it's best to start your hike somewhat cold because your body temperature will rise as you get moving. This will keep you from stopping too often to shed layers and help your body acclimate to the weather.

Lastly, hydration is as important in winter as it is during the summer. Cooler weather inhibits your thirst and it can be easy to forget to drink water. Consider setting a repeating timer on your watch or phone to remind you to hydrate regularly.

You can download this checklist in high-quality (print-ready) format at:

https://www.theadventurejunkies.com/gear-book-bonus

THE ADVENTURE JUNKIES
PACKING LIST:
WINTER DAY HIKE

Essential: You need it to go hiking
Safety: Not essential, but it increases your safety
Comfort: Not essential, but can make the hike more enjoyable

BAGS & APPAREL

	ESSENTIAL	SAFETY	COMFORT
☐ Day Pack	√		
☐ Pack Rain Cover			√
☐ Moisture-Wicking Thermal Baselayer	√		
☐ Mid-layer Fleece	√		
☐ Warm Winter Jacket	√		
☐ Quick-Drying Pants	√		
☐ Moisture-Wicking Underwear	√		
☐ Wool Socks	√		
☐ Hiking Boots	√		
☐ Rain Jacket / Waterproof Layer	√		
☐ Rain Pants			√
☐ Gaiters			√
☐ Balaclava			√
☐ Beanie / Warm Hat	√		
☐ Gloves	√		

TOOLS & ACCESSORIES

	ESSENTIAL	SAFETY	COMFORT
☐ Trekking Poles		√	√
☐ Crampons / Snow Shoes		√	
☐ Ice Axe		√	
☐ Headlamp		√	
☐ Binoculars			√
☐ Chargers		√	
☐ Knife / Multi-Tool			√
☐ Camera			√
☐ Camera Hood / Rain Cover			√
☐ Extra Batteries			√
☐ Fitness Tracker			√

NAVIGATION & COMMUNICATION

	ESSENTIAL	SAFETY	COMFORT
☐ Map / Compass		√	
☐ GPS		√	
☐ Two-Way Radio		√	
☐ PLB / Satellite Radio		√	
☐ Hiking Guide		√	
☐ Watch		√	

FOOD & WATER

	ESSENTIAL	SAFETY	COMFORT
☐ Water Bottle / Hydration Reservoir	√		
☐ Water Treatment System		√	
☐ Lunch / Snacks			√
☐ Emergency Supply of Food		√	
☐ Camping Stove			√
☐ Stove Fuel			√
☐ Matches or Lighter			√
☐ Cookware			√
☐ Cutlery			√
☐ Waste Bag	√		

SAFETY & REPAIR

	ESSENTIAL	SAFETY	COMFORT
☐ First Aid Kit		√	
☐ Lighter / Matches / Fire Starter		√	
☐ Bear Spray		√	
☐ Emergency Shelter		√	
☐ Whistle		√	
☐ Trail Route Itinerary Left With a Friend		√	

HEALTH & HYGEINE

	ESSENTIAL	SAFETY	COMFORT
☐ Sunglasses	√		
☐ Chapstick / Lip Balm			√
☐ Hand Sanitizer		√	
☐ Baby Wipes			√
☐ Rubbing Alcohol / Antiseptic Wipes		√	
☐ Prescription Medication		√	
☐ Over the Counter Medication (i.e. Aspirin)			√
☐ Toilet Paper			√
☐ Urinary Products			√
☐ Menstruation Products			√
☐ Trowel			√
☐ Blister Treatment			√

PERSONAL ITEMS

	ESSENTIAL	SAFETY	COMFORT
☐ Field Journal w/ Pen / Pencil			√
☐ Personal Identification Card		√	
☐ Cell Phone		√	
☐ Cash / Credit Card	√		
☐ Hammock			√
☐ Blanket			√

30. SUMMER OVERNIGHT HIKE

Overnight hikes can range anywhere from 8 – 28 miles roundtrip and typically take about 2 full days to accomplish. When camping overnight in the summer, gear and apparel will be some of your most important considerations.

Summer camping lends itself to simpler gear and as such many people opt for minimal shelters over tents. Bivys, hammocks, and simple tarp setups are an easy way to stay sheltered with less pack weight.

When it comes to summer apparel, keep in mind the region you'll be camping in. You won't need a fleece or jacket in the Southeastern U.S. in the summer due to warm overnight temperatures and extreme humidity. However, in drier climates such as the desert or in cooler regions like the Pacific Northwest, you will most likely need one as temperatures tend to drop at sunset.

You can download this checklist in high-quality (print-ready) format at:

https://www.theadventurejunkies.com/gear-book-bonus

THE ADVENTURE JUNKIES
PACKING LIST:
SUMMER OVERNIGHT HIKE

Essential: You need it to go hiking
Safety: Not essential, but it increases your safety
Comfort: Not essential, but can make the hike more enjoyable

BACKPACKING GEAR

	ESSENTIAL	SAFETY	COMFORT
☐ Multi-Day Pack	√		
☐ Pack Rain Cover			√
☐ Tent / Tarp / Hammock	√		
☐ Tent Footprint			√
☐ Sleeping Bag (with Stuff Sack)	√		
☐ Sleeping Bag Liner			√
☐ Compression Sack			√
☐ Sleeping Pad	√		
☐ Pillow			√

APPAREL

	ESSENTIAL	SAFETY	COMFORT
☐ Moisture-Wicking T-Shirt	√		
☐ Long Sleeve Shirt with UPF		√	√
☐ Quick-Drying Pants / Shorts	√		
☐ Lightweight Fleece or Jacket			√
☐ Moisture-Wicking Underwear	√		
☐ Sleeping Clothes			√
☐ Socks (synthetic or wool)	√		
☐ Hiking Boots / Sandals / Sneakers	√		
☐ Rain Jacket / Waterproof Layer		√	√
☐ Rain Pants			√
☐ Gaiters			√
☐ Bandana / Buff			√
☐ Sun Hat	√		

SAFETY & REPAIR

	ESSENTIAL	SAFETY	COMFORT
☐ First Aid Kit		√	
☐ Tent / Stove / Sleeping Pad Repair Kits		√	
☐ Lighter / Matches / Fire Starter		√	
☐ Bear Spray		√	
☐ Emergency Shelter		√	
☐ Whistle		√	
☐ Trail Route Itinerary Left With a Friend		√	

FOOD & WATER

	ESSENTIAL	SAFETY	COMFORT
☐ Water Bottle / Hydration Reservoir	√		
☐ Water Treatment System		√	
☐ Meals	√		
☐ Snacks / Energy Bars			√
☐ Emergency Supply of Food		√	

CAMP KITCHEN

	ESSENTIAL	SAFETY	COMFORT
☐ Camping Stove	√		
☐ Stove Fuel	√		
☐ Matches or Lighter	√		
☐ Cookware			√
☐ Plates, Bowls and Cups			√
☐ French Press			√
☐ Utensils			√
☐ Biodegradable Soap and Sponge			√
☐ Small Reusable Napkin			√
☐ Waste Bag	√		
☐ Bear Cannister / Hang Bag + 50' rope			√

HEALTH & HYGEINE

	ESSENTIAL	SAFETY	COMFORT
☐ Sunscreen	√		
☐ Sunglasses	√		
☐ Prescription Glasses / Contacts			√
☐ Chapstick / Lip Balm (w/ SPF)			√
☐ Insect Repellant			√
☐ Toothbrush / Toothpaste			√
☐ Hand Sanitizer		√	
☐ Baby Wipes			√
☐ Rubbing Alcohol / Antiseptic Wipes		√	
☐ Prescription Medication		√	
☐ Over the Counter Medication (i.e. Aspirin)			√
☐ Toilet Paper	√		
☐ Urinary Products			√
☐ Menstruation Products			√
☐ Trowel	√		
☐ Blister Treatment			√
☐ Portable Camp Shower			√

NAVIGATION & COMMUNICATION

	ESSENTIAL	SAFETY	COMFORT
☐ Map / Compass		√	
☐ GPS		√	
☐ Two-Way Radio		√	
☐ PLB / Satellite Radio		√	
☐ Hiking Guide		√	
☐ Watch		√	

TOOLS & ACCESSORIES

	ESSENTIAL	SAFETY	COMFORT
☐ Trekking Poles		√	√
☐ Headlamp	√		
☐ Backpacking Lantern			√
☐ Binoculars			√
☐ Chargers		√	
☐ Knife / Multi-Tool		√	
☐ Camera			√
☐ Camera Hood / Rain Cover			√
☐ Extra Batteries			√
☐ Portable Solar Panel			√
☐ Power Bank			√
☐ Fitness Tracker			√

PERSONAL ITEMS

	ESSENTIAL	SAFETY	COMFORT
☐ Permits (if required)	√		
☐ Field Journal w/ Pen / Pencil			√
☐ Personal Identification Card		√	
☐ Cell Phone		√	
☐ Cash / Credit Card	√		
☐ Hammock			√
☐ Camp Chair			√
☐ Playing Cards / Dice / Games			√
☐ Picnic Blanket			√

THE ADVENTURE JUNKIES

31. WINTER OVERNIGHT HIKE

Because of inclement weather and less daylight, winter overnight hikes tend to run a bit shorter than hikes in the warmer seasons and can range anywhere between 8 – 24 miles roundtrip. When camping overnight in the winter, warmth and tools will be some of your most important considerations.

When it comes to staying warm, layering clothing is hugely important as it can help you avoid/minimize sweating. Sweating too much in cold temperatures can be dangerous as it can lower your body temperature and make you even colder. Consider a puffy down jacket for your outer layer – it will help pull moisture away from your body. Also, having an extra pair of wool socks at night is imperative as it will allow your hiking socks to properly dry.

Your gear should also be winter specific, such as high R-value sleeping pads, 4-season tents, and appropriate winter temperature sleeping bags. In addition to needing tools that will help you tackle a snowy trail (i.e. crampons, trekking poles, snowshoes, or an ice axe), consider other winter specific supplies. Keep in mind that liquid fuel (white gas) stoves tend to perform better than Butane canister stoves in extreme cold.

You can download this checklist in high-quality (print-ready) format at:

https://www.theadventurejunkies.com/gear-book-bonus

THE ADVENTURE JUNKIES

PACKING LIST:
WINTER OVERNIGHT HIKE

Essential: You need it to go hiking
Safety: Not essential, but it increases your safety
Comfort: Not essential, but can make the hike more enjoyable

BACKPACKING GEAR

	Essential	Safety	Comfort
Multi-Day Pack	√		
Pack Rain Cover			√
4-Season Tent	√		
Tent Footprint			√
Winter Rated Sleeping Bag	√		
Sleeping Bag Liner			√
Compression Sack			√
Sleeping Pad	√		
Pillow			√

APPAREL

	Essential	Safety	Comfort
Moisture-Wicking Thermal Baselayer	√		
Mid-layer Fleece	√		
Warm Winter Jacket	√		
Quick-Drying Pants	√		
Moisture-Wicking Underwear	√		
Thermal Leggings	√		
Sleeping Clothes			√
Wool Socks	√		
Extra Pair of Wool Socks	√		
Hiking Boots	√		
Rain Jacket / Waterproof Layer	√		
Rain Pants	√		
Gaiters			√
Balaclava			√
Beanie / Warm Hat	√		
Gloves	√		
Waterproof Shell Gloves			√
Hand / Foot Warmers			√

FOOD & WATER

	Essential	Safety	Comfort
Water Bottle / Hydration Reservoir	√		
Water Treatment System		√	
Meals	√		
Snacks / Energy Bars			√
Emergency Supply of Food		√	

TOOLS & ACCESSORIES

	Essential	Safety	Comfort
Trekking Poles		√	√
Crampons / Snow Shoes		√	
Ice Axe		√	
Headlamp	√		
Backpacking Lantern			√
Binoculars			√
Chargers		√	
Knife / Multi-Tool		√	
Camera			√
Camera Hood / Rain Cover			√
Extra Batteries			√
Portable Solar Panel			√
Power Bank			√
Fitness Tracker			√

CAMP KITCHEN

	Essential	Safety	Comfort
Camping Stove	√		
Stove Fuel	√		
Matches or Lighter	√		
Cookware			√
Plates, Bowls and Cups			√
French Press			√
Utensils			√
Biodegradable Soap and Sponge			√
Small Reusable Napkin			√
Waste Bag	√		
Bear Cannister / Hang Bag + 50' rope			√

SAFETY & REPAIR

	Essential	Safety	Comfort
First Aid Kit	√		
Tent / Stove / Sleeping Pad Repair Kits	√		
Lighter / Matches / Fire Starter	√		
Bear Spray		√	
Emergency Shelter / Space Blanket	√		
Whistle		√	
Trail Route Itinerary Left With a Friend		√	

NAVIGATION & COMMUNICATION	ESSENTIAL	SAFETY	COMFORT
☐ Map / Compass		√	
☐ GPS		√	
☐ Two-Way Radio		√	
☐ PLB / Satellite Radio		√	
☐ Hiking Guide		√	
☐ Watch		√	

HEALTH & HYGEINE	ESSENTIAL	SAFETY	COMFORT
☐ Sunglasses	√		
☐ Prescription Glasses / Contacts			√
☐ Chapstick / Lip Balm (w/ SPF)			√
☐ Toothbrush / Toothpaste			√
☐ Hand Sanitizer		√	
☐ Baby Wipes			√
☐ Rubbing Alcohol / Antiseptic Wipes		√	
☐ Prescription Medication		√	
☐ Over the Counter Medication (i.e. Aspirin)			√
☐ Toilet Paper	√		
☐ Urinary Products			√
☐ Menstruation Products			√
☐ Trowel	√		
☐ Blister Treatment			√
☐ Portable Camp Shower			√

PERSONAL ITEMS	ESSENTIAL	SAFETY	COMFORT
☐ Permits (if required)	√		
☐ Field Journal w/ Pen / Pencil			√
☐ Personal Identification Card		√	
☐ Cell Phone		√	
☐ Cash / Credit Card	√		
☐ Hammock			√
☐ Camp Chair			√
☐ Playing Cards / Dice / Games			√
☐ Blanket			√

THE ADVENTURE JUNKIES

32. SUMMER MULTI-DAY HIKE

Multi-day hikes can vary widely depending on how many days you'll be in the wilderness. During the summer, you can reasonably expect to hike about 10 – 12 miles per day with thru-hikers and ambitious backpackers pushing that range to 15 – 20 miles per day.

When backpacking for multiple days in the summer, your focus should be on planning your resources to optimize your body over several days or weeks. Lighter gear and the appropriate tools are paramount.

Streamlining your gear for lighter travel makes a huge difference when trekking multiple days. As the miles add up, a lighter load means less fatigue. Consider minimalist shelters and try to be pickier about what you choose to bring.

Also be mindful of taking care of your body by having the proper tools. Your feet will appreciate having moleskins for blister care and having a reliable method of treating water will keep you well hydrated.

You can download this checklist in high-quality (print-ready) format at:

https://www.theadventurejunkies.com/gear-book-bonus

THE ADVENTURE JUNKIES

PACKING LIST:
SUMMER MULTI-DAY HIKE

Essential: You need it to go hiking
Safety: Not essential, but it increases your safety
Comfort: Not essential, but can make the hike more enjoyable

BACKPACKING GEAR

	Essential	Safety	Comfort
☐ Multi-Day Pack	✓		
☐ Pack Rain Cover			✓
☐ Day Pack			✓
☐ Tent / Tarp / Hammock	✓		
☐ Tent Footprint			✓
☐ Sleeping Bag (with Stuff Sack)	✓		
☐ Sleeping Bag Liner			✓
☐ Compression Sack			✓
☐ Sleeping Pad	✓		
☐ Pillow			✓

APPAREL

	Essential	Safety	Comfort
☐ Moisture-Wicking T-Shirt	✓		
☐ Long Sleeve Shirt with UPF		✓	✓
☐ Quick-Drying Pants / Shorts	✓		
☐ Lightweight Fleece or Jacket			✓
☐ Moisture-Wicking Underwear	✓		
☐ Sleeping Clothes			✓
☐ Socks (Synthetic or Wool)	✓		
☐ Extra Pair of Socks			✓
☐ Hiking Boots / Sandals	✓		
☐ Rain Jacket / Waterproof Layer		✓	✓
☐ Rain Pants			✓
☐ Gaiters			✓
☐ Bandana/Buff			✓
☐ Sun Hat	✓		

SAFETY & REPAIR

	Essential	Safety	Comfort
☐ First Aid Kit	✓		
☐ Tent / Stove / Sleeping Pad Repair Kits	✓		
☐ Lighter / Matches / Fire Starter	✓		
☐ Bear Spray		✓	
☐ Emergency Shelter		✓	
☐ Whistle		✓	
☐ Trail Route Itinerary Left With a Friend		✓	

FOOD & WATER

	Essential	Safety	Comfort
☐ Water Bottle / Hydration Reservoir	✓		
☐ Water Treatment System		✓	
☐ Meals	✓		
☐ Snacks / Energy Bars			✓
☐ Emergency Supply of Food		✓	

CAMP KITCHEN

	Essential	Safety	Comfort
☐ Camping Stove	✓		
☐ Stove Fuel	✓		
☐ Matches or Lighter	✓		
☐ Cookware			✓
☐ Plates, Bowls and Cups			✓
☐ French Press			✓
☐ Utensils			✓
☐ Biodegradable Soap and Sponge			✓
☐ Small Reusable Napkin			✓
☐ Waste Bag	✓		
☐ Bear Cannister / Hang Bag + 50' rope			✓

HEALTH & HYGEINE

	Essential	Safety	Comfort
☐ Sunscreen	✓		
☐ Sunglasses	✓		
☐ Prescription Glasses / Contacts			✓
☐ Chapstick / Lip Balm (w/ SPF)			✓
☐ Insect Repellant			✓
☐ Toothbrush / Toothpaste			✓
☐ Hand Sanitizer		✓	
☐ Baby Wipes			✓
☐ Rubbing Alcohol / Antiseptic Wipes		✓	
☐ Prescription Medication		✓	
☐ Over the Counter Medication (i.e. Aspirin)			✓
☐ Toilet Paper	✓		
☐ Urinary Products			✓
☐ Menstruation Products			✓
☐ Trowel	✓		
☐ Blister Treatment			✓
☐ Portable Camp Shower			✓

NAVIGATION & COMMUNICATION

	ESSENTIAL	SAFETY	COMFORT
☐ Map / Compass		√	
☐ GPS		√	
☐ Two-Way Radio		√	
☐ PLB / Satellite Radio		√	
☐ Hiking Guide		√	
☐ Watch		√	

TOOLS & ACCESSORIES

	ESSENTIAL	SAFETY	COMFORT
☐ Trekking Poles		√	√
☐ Headlamp	√		
☐ Spare Batteries for Headlamp			√
☐ Backpacking Lantern			√
☐ Binoculars			√
☐ Chargers		√	
☐ Knife / Multi-Tool		√	
☐ Camera			√
☐ Camera Hood / Rain Cover			√
☐ Extra Batteries			√
☐ Portable Solar Panel			√
☐ Power Bank			√
☐ Fitness Tracker			√

PERSONAL ITEMS

	ESSENTIAL	SAFETY	COMFORT
☐ Permits (if required)	√		
☐ Field Journal w/ Pen / Pencil			√
☐ Personal Identification Card		√	
☐ Cell Phone		√	
☐ Cash / Credit Card	√		
☐ Hammock			√
☐ Camp Chair			√
☐ Playing Cards / Dice / Games			√
☐ Picnic Blanket			√

THE ADVENTURE JUNKIES

33. WINTER MULTI-DAY HIKE

Tackling a multi-day hike in wintery and potentially inclement weather may seem daunting, but with the right amount of pre-planning, it is very manageable. Daily distances tend to be shorter than during summer since there's less daylight and winter multi-day packs tend to be heavier.

Having the proper tools, bringing strategic clothing, and planning meals will ensure your success. A collapsible shovel will give you the ability to dig into a snowy area and create a kitchen shelter separate from your tent. You can use a snowbank to build a table with seating in the kitchen space or even make an igloo!

Gloves, beanies, and head covers are incredibly important while hiking overnight in the winter as they are an easy way to regulate body temperature without having to stop and remove layers. Multiple pairs of wool socks are also vital for staying warm and dry.

Lastly, planning meals and staying well hydrated will also ensure a successful multi-day hike during winter. Freeze-dried meals are an easy way to make sure you're getting enough calories to complete the hike and stay warm while doing it.

You can download this checklist in high-quality (print-ready) format at:

https://www.theadventurejunkies.com/gear-book-bonus

THE ADVENTURE JUNKIES
PACKING LIST:
WINTER MULTI-DAY HIKE

Essential: You need it to go hiking
Safety: Not essential, but it increases your safety
Comfort: Not essential, but can make the hike more enjoyable

BACKPACKING GEAR

	ESSENTIAL	SAFETY	COMFORT
☐ Multi-Day Pack	√		
☐ Pack Rain Cover			√
☐ Day Pack			√
☐ Tent	√		
☐ Tent Footprint			√
☐ Sleeping Bag (with Stuff Sack)	√		
☐ Sleeping Bag Liner			√
☐ Compression Sack			√
☐ Sleeping Pad	√		
☐ Pillow			√

APPAREL

	ESSENTIAL	SAFETY	COMFORT
☐ Moisture-Wicking Thermal Baselayer	√		
☐ Mid-layer Fleece	√		
☐ Warm Winter Jacket	√		
☐ Quick-Drying Pants	√		
☐ Moisture-Wicking Underwear	√		
☐ Thermal Leggings	√		
☐ Sleeping Clothes			√
☐ Wool Socks	√		
☐ Extra Wool Socks (2-3 Pairs)	√		
☐ Hiking Boots	√		
☐ Rain Jacket / Waterproof Layer	√		
☐ Rain Pants	√		
☐ Gaiters			√
☐ Balaclava			√
☐ Beanie / Warm Hat	√		
☐ Gloves	√		
☐ Hand / Foot Warmers			√

FOOD & WATER

	ESSENTIAL	SAFETY	COMFORT
☐ Water Bottle / Hydration Reservoir	√		
☐ Water Treatment System		√	
☐ Meals	√		
☐ Snacks / Energy Bars			√
☐ Emergency Supply of Food	√		

TOOLS & ACCESSORIES

	ESSENTIAL	SAFETY	COMFORT
☐ Trekking Poles		√	√
☐ Crampons / Snow Shoes		√	
☐ Ice Axe		√	
☐ Collapsible Shovel			√
☐ Headlamp	√		
☐ Spare Batteries For Headlamp		√	
☐ Backpacking Lantern			√
☐ Binoculars			√
☐ Chargers		√	
☐ Knife / Multi-Tool		√	
☐ Camera			√
☐ Camera Hood / Rain Cover			√
☐ Extra Batteries			√
☐ Portable Solar Panel			√
☐ Power Bank			√
☐ Fitness Tracker			√

CAMP KITCHEN

	ESSENTIAL	SAFETY	COMFORT
☐ Camping Stove	√		
☐ Stove Fuel	√		
☐ Matches or Lighter	√		
☐ Cookware			√
☐ Plates, Bowls and Cups			√
☐ French Press			√
☐ Utensils			√
☐ Biodegradable Soap and Sponge			√
☐ Small Reusable Napkin			√
☐ Waste Bag	√		
☐ Bear Cannister / Hang Bag + 50' rope			√

SAFETY & REPAIR

	ESSENTIAL	SAFETY	COMFORT
☐ First Aid Kit	√		
☐ Tent / Stove / Sleeping Pad Repair Kits	√		
☐ Lighter / Matches / Fire Starter	√		
☐ Bear Spray		√	
☐ Emergency Shelter / Space Blanket	√		
☐ Whistle		√	
☐ Trail Route Itinerary Left With a Friend		√	

NAVIGATION & COMMUNICATION

	ESSENTIAL	SAFETY	COMFORT
☐ Map / Compass		√	
☐ GPS		√	
☐ Two-Way Radio		√	
☐ PLB / Satellite Radio		√	
☐ Hiking Guide		√	
☐ Watch		√	

HEALTH & HYGEINE

	ESSENTIAL	SAFETY	COMFORT
☐ Sunglasses	√		
☐ Prescription Glasses / Contacts	√		
☐ Chapstick / Lip Balm (w/ SPF)			√
☐ Toothbrush / Toothpaste			√
☐ Hand Sanitizer		√	
☐ Baby Wipes			√
☐ Rubbing Alcohol / Antiseptic Wipes		√	
☐ Prescription Medication		√	
☐ Over the Counter Medication (i.e. Aspirin)			√
☐ Toilet Paper	√		
☐ Urinary Products			√
☐ Menstruation Products			√
☐ Trowel	√		
☐ Blister Treatment			√
☐ Portable Camp Shower			√

PERSONAL ITEMS

	ESSENTIAL	SAFETY	COMFORT
☐ Permits (if required)	√		
☐ Field Journal w/ Pen / Pencil			√
☐ Personal Identification Card		√	
☐ Cell Phone		√	
☐ Cash / Credit Card	√		
☐ Hammock			√
☐ Camp Chair			√
☐ Playing Cards / Dice / Games			√
☐ Blanket			√

THE ADVENTURE JUNKIES

WRITE A REVIEW

We truly value your feedback!

We'd love to hear what you
thought about the book.

Scan the QR code below and go to Amazon
now, so you can leave us an honest review.

NEXT STEPS

If you love the outdoors and can't live without adventure in your life, these are the next steps we recommend taking:

Join the Summit Community

Summit is a free online community that brings together educational content, video, live events and community—all in one place. It's like Facebook for adventure junkies, but with better privacy, no ads and tons of extras.

summit.theadventurejunkies.com

Subscribe to Friday Fix

Friday Fix is a weekly email with the top handpicked tools, tips and recommendations for living a bold and adventurous life. No charge. No spam. Unsubscribe anytime.

www.theadventurejunkies.com/friday-fix

Subscribe to ReWild Magazine

ReWild is the go-to digital destination for adventure junkies who are craving a more profound connection to nature, to wild places, wild animals, and their wild-selves. We help our readers live an adventurous and intentional life that is in alignment with the natural world.

ReWild focuses on individuals who are actively searching for ways to live in harmony with nature. Our magazine not only motivates and inspires our readers to listen to their own wild calling, but we also provide them with the tools, products and information to make their dreams come to life.

www.rewildmagazine.com

Get Your Adventure Pass

Never pay full price again. With Adventure Pass you can access thousands of discounts on outdoor gear & experiences worldwide.

www.theadventurepass.com

BOOKS IN THIS SERIES

The Adventure Junkies Hiking Series

The Beginner's Guide To Outdoor Clothing

Learn what to wear while hiking so you stay safe and comfortable in any weather condition.

The Ultimate Guide To Hiking For Older Adults

Learn how to avoid, treat and prevent different pains and other age-related issues when hiking.

ABOUT THE AUTHOR

Jonathan Dufner

Jonathan Dufner carries a wide range of experience and hiking knowledge with a special talent of understanding beginners. He has led countless groups into the wilderness and has taught a variety of outdoor skills clinics.

ABOUT THE ADVENTURE JUNKIES

The Adventure Junkies' mission is to make the outdoors accessible to everyone in order to inspire people to value, understand and protect our planet's ecosystems.

We believe when you step out into the wild places of the world, you don't come back the same person. Experiences in nature inspire a lifelong connection with our planet and the creatures we share it with. We do what we do, because we believe the world needs more adventure junkies.

An adventure junkie is much more than someone who's addicted to adventure. They are infinite learners, dreamers, and doers. They set big goals for themselves and push their limits to achieve them. Through their experiences in the outdoors, they've developed a deep sense of respect for nature.

To help people become adventure junkies, we created this website to be THE place to go to learn about outdoor activities and connect with a global network of like-minded people. Through our actionable digital resources and our supportive online communities, we give you the tools you need to experience nature in powerful ways.

Whether you dream of hiking through a pristine forest or exploring the depths of the ocean, we're here to help make it possible.

We do all this because we believe in the power of adventure. We believe that getting people out into nature is THE solution to lasting conservation of the world's species and ecosystems.

Conservation is a state of harmony between humans, the land and all living creatures. It's about balance, respect, and understanding. Conservation efforts create a world where all life can coexist and thrive for generations to come. Experiences outdoors inspire this harmony like nothing else. Films, books, and T.V shows can certainly spark an interest, but nothing compares to the experience itself. You have to be there. You have to see it, to feel it to understand how precious nature is.

Stepping outdoors creates a chain of events. First, it empowers the adventurer with a new perspective. Second, it provides jobs for local communities. Third, it demonstrates the value of wildlife and natural ecosystems to government leaders.

As a company, The Adventure Junkies has a role to play in making a positive impact in conservation. We want to help you explore our beautiful planet today!

Sounds like something you'd like to be a part of? Here's what you can do.

1) Use our resources: The Adventure Junkies offers the best tools to learn a new outdoor activity on the web. Access all of our learning resources at www.theadventurejunkies.com/library

2) Join Summit: People just like you are using Summit to improve their outdoor skills, connect with other passionate outdoor lovers, and to become a safer and more confident outdoorsman (or woman). You can join Summit at summit.theadventurejunkies.com

3) Go on an adventure!: Once you're geared up and ready to go, turn off your screen and get outside.

PHOTO CREDITS

Summer Day Hike: https://www.istockphoto.com/portfolio/m-imagephotography

Winter Day Hike: https://www.istockphoto.com/portfolio/shironosov

Summer Overnight Hike: https://www.istockphoto.com/portfolio/rawpixel

Winter Overnight Hike: https://www.istockphoto.com/portfolio/olga_danylenko

Summer Multi-day Hike: https://www.istockphoto.com/portfolio/yulkapopkova

Winter Multi-day Hike: https://www.istockphoto.com/portfolio/blyjak

Day Packs: https://www.istockphoto.com/portfolio/CEBImagery

Multi-day Packs: https://www.istockphoto.com/portfolio/lzf

Tents: https://www.istockphoto.com/portfolio/kwiktor

Sleeping Bags: https://www.istockphoto.com/portfolio/Ross-Helen

Sleeping Bag Liners: https://www.istockphoto.com/portfolio/Solovyova

Sleeping Pads: https://www.istockphoto.com/portfolio/Everste

Stoves: https://www.istockphoto.com/portfolio/PichitchaiJampasri

Cookware: https://www.istockphoto.com/portfolio/MaximFesenko

Utensils: https://www.istockphoto.com/portfolio/kurgu128

Cleaning Items: https://www.istockphoto.com/portfolio/kievith

Water Storage: https://www.istockphoto.com/portfolio/gaspr13

Water Treatment Systems: https://www.istockphoto.com/portfolio/eppicphotography

Compasses: https://www.istockphoto.com/portfolio/markonikolicphoto

GPS: https://www.istockphoto.com/portfolio/sanderstock

Watches: https://www.istockphoto.com/portfolio/lzf

Hiking Poles: https://www.istockphoto.com/portfolio/abadonian

Headlamps: https://www.istockphoto.com/portfolio/anatoliy_gleb

Binoculars: https://www.istockphoto.com/portfolio/rawpixel

Chargers: https://www.istockphoto.com/portfolio/Diy13

Knives & Multi-tools: https://www.istockphoto.com/portfolio/spaxiax

Cameras: https://www.istockphoto.com/portfolio/yarygin

First Aid Kits: https://www.istockphoto.com/portfolio/eurobanks

Foot Care: https://www.istockphoto.com/portfolio/patrickpoendl

Repair Kits: https://www.istockphoto.com/es/portfolio/bernardbodo

Communication Devices: https://www.istockphoto.com/portfolio/staswalenga

Camp Bathrooms: https://www.istockphoto.com/portfolio/4nadia

Female Hygiene: https://www.istockphoto.com/portfolio/maridav